PARENTING WITH
GUMPTION AND GRIT

PARENTING WITH GUMPTION AND GRIT

52 Must-Read Parenting Tips for Anyone who has
Ever Loved a Child Enough to Want to
Influence Their Future

Judy McCarver

ELM HILL

A Division of
HarperCollins Christian Publishing

www.elmhillbooks.com

Parenting with Gumption and Grit
52 Must-Read Parenting Tips for Anyone who has
Ever Loved a Child Enough to Want to Influence Their Future

Published in Nashville, Tennessee, by Elm Hill, an imprint of Thomas Nelson. Elm Hill and Thomas Nelson are registered trademarks of HarperCollins Christian Publishing, Inc.

Elm Hill titles may be purchased in bulk for educational, business, fund-raising, or sales promotional use. For information, please e-mail SpecialMarkets@ ThomasNelson.com.

Library of Congress Cataloging-in-Publication Data

Library of Congress Control Number: 2019931080

ISBN 978-1-595559449 (Paperback)
ISBN 978-1-595559562 (eBook)

The wild and crazy, seemingly overwhelming, often precarious, delicate and rough, long and short, frightening and courageous, gut-wrenching sad, but overflowing with joy and adventure of *Parenting with Gumption and Grit!*

This book is dedicated to my three daughters,
Shelby Carrol, Halle Kristine, and Katie Ann.
I love you all three so very much, and you are truly the
measure of God's grace in my life.

TABLE OF CONTENTS

FOREWORD

Once in a Sunday morning lesson, my pastor said to all of us sitting there listening, "What keeps you awake at night? And what can you do about it?" In other words, if you are wondering where your *COM*passions and your passions lie, if you know there is *SOME*thing you should be doing to contribute, but not sure what that is, ask yourself that question: "What keeps you awake at night?" Okay, yeah, besides your little guy asking for the 150th time for a drink of water, what else? Well, undoubtedly for me it had something to do with parenting. Taking these precious little ones with whom we have been dearly entrusted and somehow, someway, moving them to become not just "happy" adults, but world-changing, compassionate, capable, and contributing adults. But how?

As I moved from one season to the other in parenting—infancy, toddler age, elementary age, puberty, teens, and young adulthood—it became painfully obvious to me that the challenges often eclipsed the support we have in our lives to do just that. Resources abound. We live in an information age, and yet I saw over and over again that parents were "goin' it alone," as if to say, "I've got this." We pay hundreds of thousands of dollars to universities and other educational institutions to learn our trades. Moreover, we pay thousands upon thousands to give our kids the proper instruction they need to be successful in extracurricular activities and in their schools. We do *THAT* because we know "*I ain't got this.*" I can't teach my kid piano or dance or football or karate. For that, I have to have instruction. Yet here we are, parents of a brand-new human being—scariest thing ever. But we hesitate to admit, "This might be the area of my life where I most need to seek out sound, logical, and loving instruction, or listen to others with credibility who have gone before (with an open spirit and eager mind) to find out how to avoid the inevitable pitfalls that will challenge me in perhaps the most challenging job I will ever do in my entire life: parenting."

I am not going to lie. Along with this passion, there stirred up in me a discontent with a lot of what I saw in parenting in this materialistic, performance-driven culture in which we live: America. A righteous indignation on the part of children began to grow inside of me. I couldn't contain it. It spilled out into my conversations, my blog, and greatly impacted my own parenting. (Bless my children—they have received healthy doses of my righteous indignation.) I have teetered on the edge of being judgmental of parents versus being tolerant of their different parenting styles. And I dare say, sometimes, I have jumped the fence completely. I have begged forgiveness and have been forgiven. But all of that has led me to this project. Initially, I thought I would just post a daily parenting tip on Facebook. And I did, about ten of them. I had a lot of positive feedback from (gracious) friends who said things like, "This was really helpful to me," or, "You should write a book," and the one that I liked the best: "If you do write a book, I'll buy it." Bonus! I did some self-reflection, along with a lot of prayerful consideration, and decided that the reason I couldn't get this OFF my mind could mean it's taken up residence there.

My qualifications for writing this book are clearly not due to all of my unprecedented successes as a parent. Nor is it attached to a voluminous number of college degrees and dissertations. But rather, it is based on my many and varied parenting fails over the years with just enough successes peppered throughout to keep me keepin' on. And my ability to learn from my mistakes as well as from the mistakes of others. This is my attempt to make a small difference. So use it or lose it parents (and those of you parenting by mentoring or fostering). I hope you use it. I sincerely hope you see the heart from which it springs. One that loves and cherishes young people, one who loves her own enough to grow them into women capable of leaving their dad and me behind, to go out into a big, huge, hurting world and make a powerful difference, and yes, even be self-fulfilled in the process.

So sure, write a book about parenting. And toss it in the pile among a million others written by people with a lot more acronyms behind their names than mine. I thought about a signature block with BS behind it for my bachelor of science, but I was too afraid that acronym might be confused for something else. Then I thought I could sign off with MPA. I do have a master's degree in public administration, but no one knows what the heck that is or what it has to do with anything, let alone parenting. But it occurred to me that one of the "qualifiers" lending itself to my writing this book are all of those experiences that have *brought me* to this point and have served to ignite this passion in me. A few of those include my parents' death in a fishing accident when I was at the young age of five, and the ensuing challenges that followed me for the rest of my childhood and into young adulthood, the deaths of five coworkers and many other colleagues in a despicable act of domestic terrorism in the 1995 bombing of the Oklahoma City Alfred P. Murrah Federal Building, just a year before I became a parent myself.

Moreover, as a young mom, I endured long deployments alone with our kids, separated from my husband, compliments of the United States Air Force. He was an active duty pilot for twenty-three years. He went from that career to a second one flying for a commercial airline. I have known the toil that comes from being at home alone with your children, albeit physically, not emotionally. Through the grace of God, and in spite of some difficult seasons in my life, we have raised three kind, compassionate, and productive young women. We have made mistakes along the way but have never given up. We continue to strive to "do the next right thing" (Tip #44). We have tried to be transparent in our own realities of both marriage and parenting. These varying life experiences, professional and personal, has lent itself to more effective parenting and also the unusual ability to meet people (parents) right where they are in their life and in their parenting.

In view of all of this, I realized that the best acronym I could place at the end of my signature block would be: "Been there. Done that. Trying to Do What's Best." So that's that. I'm someone with a lot of passion, a combination of professional and personal experience (both joyful and sad), writing about a subject that fills my heart with a sense of urgency—one that I want to spread like fire among the masses of people who bear the title "Parent" or "Mentor." READ ON!

The Real and True Definition of Parenting and Mentoring

Parenting should never be attributed to us in title only. It's certainly also a role. I am married to a pilot, and a retiree of the United States Air Force. At just about any American air base in this country and abroad, you will see wonderful static displays of different aircrafts. We can see and read the title of the aircraft and find out more about it from the placard erected there. But these aircrafts are a static display only, which means you cannot climb in and go for a ride. But their *role—their place—*in our history is colorful and exciting, and was once critical to our country's defense. Likewise, a title such as parent or accountant or lawyer is only a *static display* of who we are. On the other hand, a role embodies all the actions that are inherent *in* that title. Like our titles as teacher, spouse, engineer, banker, professor, or nurse—*parent* is equally important a title that embodies an exceedingly important role. Perhaps you are one who has fallen into the trap of relegating your role as a parent way down to the bottom of the title food chain. True, we do not want to lead child-centered lives (Tip #19). That's very unhealthy for parent and child, and that is not what it means to prioritize your role as a parent over all others. What it *does* mean: believing your "job" as a parent to be as important as any other "job" you have. For Pete's sake, we are rearing children into adults and moving them out into the world as workers, spouses, friends, neighbors, and voters, where they are either going to impact people and their communities in a negative way or in a positive way. Once they are adults, they are legally responsible for their own actions, or lack thereof. But between now and then, what responsibility and opportunity *does* lie at our doorstep? It's so important that we recognize relegating our parenting responsibilities to an area of unimportance renders us culpable and willing participants in a pattern of behavior in our children that may (in the very least) not be very positive, but (in the very worst case) could also be very destructive. So let's dig a little bit deeper into what makes us an effective and loving parent or mentor. Let's try to unpack this idea in perhaps an overly simplistic way: by considering *fifty-two parenting tips*—some *crucial and some optional*; however, *ALL achievable* tips that you may adopt or employ as you navigate and negotiate this fun, challenging, and crazy journey. But first, I want to outline two guiding principles I feel are necessary in order to fully embrace and engage all of the parenting tips found in the ensuing pages of this book: the principle of "connect the dots" and the "principle of faith."

The Principle of Connect the Dots

Many of us, either as children or adults, have done a coloring paper or an art project by *connecting the dots*. The object of the game is to take a pen, pencil, or crayon and connect the dots, which is usually done by drawing a line from number to number or letter to letter in either numerical or alphabetical order. Once you have connected all the dots in front of you, a complete picture of *something*, an animal, an American president, or perhaps a nature scene unfolds before your eyes. Whatever you could not see on the paper when it was first laid before you, comes into full view once all the dots are connected. Raising kids, although not nearly so easy, is a lot like that connect-the-dot art project. Each dot represents either the age of your child, a season of your life with them, significant events (deaths, marriages, funerals, weddings, graduations) as well as seemingly insignificant events (dinner around the kitchen table, family movies, holidays, birthdays). Also represented by the "dots" in our child's life would be actions *we have or have not taken* with our daughter or son, such as discipline, expressions of emotions, and personal engagement of any kind—good or bad. The dots represent any event, contact, or lack thereof that has occurred in your child's life, from infancy to young adulthood and beyond, from the time they are wholly dependent upon us for food, sustenance, and life, to the time they are fully self-sufficient. Along that colorful spectrum, we get to navigate and negotiate a lot of choices that will serve to bring our kids from the first dot of infancy to that last dot of (let's say) young adulthood. Because by that time, we certainly hope all thrusters are engaged, and they are very near spreading their wings and clearing the coop. (Flying the coop is dependent upon *clearing the coop on take-off* [Tips #21-22]).

One of the most common, yet most detrimental, mistakes we are susceptible to as parents is *not connecting those dots*. It's important to understand that what we do with them at two years old directly impacts their behavior at four, six, twelve, and twenty years old. If we fail to make those connections, the results can be devastating. Don't disconnect any year of their life with what's remaining. Too often as parents of little kids (and big), we compartmentalize their stages of growth and maturity as if one is wholly separate from the other. As a very good general rule, if you have a child with 0 responsibilities, chores, or expectations, he may become an adult who is unemployed or else an employee whose mediocrity is reflected in his appraisals and work performance. If you raise a child whose world is self-serving and self-entitled, she may well become a self-entitled spouse and employee, perhaps unwilling to bring 100 percent of their own effort to anything. If you raise children who never volunteer their efforts or resources by serving or giving to someone in need, you may well produce adults who are superficial and have little compassion for others, whether it's the indigent of our society or your child's very own next-door neighbor. If you never teach your three-, four-, or five-year-old child to respect their mom, then it is doubtful they'll respect her when he is twelve, sixteen, or twenty years old. **This concept does not mean that every single moment of your life with your kid has to be (or will be) centered on a profound life lesson. Life is busy. Some days as parents, it's all we can do to get from morning to night, and lay our head down on the pillow with our sanity intact and our children unhurt. Truth! What this concept *DOES* mean is that the <u>sum</u> of our parenting efforts inevitably <u>contributes</u> to the <u>complete</u> picture of this person we are raising.**

All of the events, at all of these different ages and stages of their lives, eventually merge together and manifests itself in a decision your child makes at a later season in life. Case in point: when our girls were little, we had a rule. You must finish what you started. If you're in the middle of soccer season and decide soccer is not for you, fine! But "you have committed to the organization, the team, and the coaches, and you *will* finish the season." I still remember a conversation I overheard between a dad and our girls' ballet teacher while waiting on my own (young) daughters to finish their class. It was literally two weeks before recital. Choreography was finished. Dance partners were assigned, and at this point, their participation critical to said choreography. This is what "Dad" said to our ballet teacher. "We (he and his wife) promised her (pampered and soon to be self-entitled daughter) she could quit either ballet or tap." (Parentheses mine.) In summary, after she had been committed for an entire semester to this ballet recital by her own choice or that of her parents, Dad and Mom were willing coconspirators in enabling her to back out of her commitment. *NOT* due to illness or family emergency. No indeed—just because "Princess" did not want to do ballet after all. I still remember the crestfallen look on our ballet teacher's face. At this point in the game, any dancer falling out of the lineup naturally catapulted her into crisis mode. Later, she told me, "It. Happens. Every. Year."

What? In our mind's eye, my husband and I saw girls who could not stay committed to a marriage or a job or a friend or a high school math assignment. *Connecting the dots* is so important in understanding that what you do or do not do with your child in the present has a monumental effect on what they do or do not do in the future. I know that's blunt, and in this highly sensitive and politically correct world in which we live, sometimes holding one another accountable is not the popular choice—that is to say, until someone's actions hurt us *personally*. Then we're all about holding someone accountable. Well, it behooves us to understand that as we parent, if we "begin with the end in mind,"[1] we are more likely to make better-informed decisions along the way. And remember, this isn't all about the negative stuff you don't want your children to become. It's also (and more) about the *joy and the delight* you want them to become. Bottom line, if your child has a certain pattern of behavior (good or bad, constructive or destructive), then embrace it or discourage it, respectively. Those behavior patterns (left checked or unchecked) will absolutely characterize the rest of their lives. ***So then, as you read through the tips in this book, wherever you see this icon: ♥, I want the "lightbulb" in your head to pop on as you take note of this particular guiding principle and think,* connect the dots applies here.** By choosing to *connect those dots*, we CAN break negative cycles in perhaps generations of families. We choose!

The Principle of Faith

Many of you, like me, are guided by your faith in your Creator. I am a Jesus follower, but unlike what the world may tell you, we aren't all bad. In fact, I dare say it is just the opposite. The Christians *I know* and surround myself with are loving, compassionate, and generous people. They are people who influence my children and help us to bring them up to be likewise loving, compassionate, and generous people themselves. My faith has been paramount in any life success I may have enjoyed up to this point. Not the least of which is parenting. But here's the thing. I don't want you to dismiss my advice in this book based on my profession of faith. I don't want you to adopt the attitude that "This doesn't apply to me because I am not a Christian." Or "This doesn't apply to me because I don't practice *any* religion."

That could not be farther from the truth. There is not a single solitary tip in this book that doesn't apply to you if you are a parent of a child or a grandparent or a mentor or a foster parent, or an adult role model. There is not a single shred of truth in the belief that Christians and non-Christians do not have the same charge in parenting and, as well, the very same challenges.

Every single tip in this book is submerged in both sense and practicality. Every tip is sprung from the same heart that loves kids and cares about what happens to them. I love your kids. I don't know them, but I love them. When I walked into a classroom at school (where I often substitute taught), I looked into those faces of those students and wondered, *Who is in their corner? Do they have anyone in their corner? Is there someone in their life who loves them so much that they are willing to discipline them, willing to sacrifice for them, willing to love them when they feel unlovable? Is there someone in their life who loves them so much that they are willing to die for them?*

Sometimes I sense the answer to that is precarious for some of these kids. *That* is what you need to know and understand when reading this book. I wrote this with your child's best interest at heart. It's with that knowledge in hand, I would like for you to step into this book and take a look around. Please read it and see if anything is helpful. I sincerely think you will find that there is much that can be applied in your parenting journey. And on the other hand, if you are a faith-filled person, you will find that your faith applies to every tip contained in this book. *So then, please note that wherever you see this:* 🙏, *the praying hands are there to direct you to a biblical reference that directly applies to that tip!* Please don't miss what your Bible has to say when it comes to the most important job we have: parenting. It is rich with spiritual principles that preempt the human expectations we have for our kids. The two can then bind together in order to impress upon our children the importance of our expectations, in a way that transcends our own abilities as parents to do so on our own.

SMART PARENTING CHOICES:
TIPS #1–13

Don't Go at It Alone; Do Surround Yourself with Helpers

Even if you are a single parent, surround yourself with sensible, loving parent friends, especially if you are the single parent of an opposite-sex child who needs that gender modeled for them. And if you are married parents, be really good friends with other married parents who encourage you and aren't afraid to tell you the truth. Thankfully, my parenting friends don't treat me with kid gloves. They know the real me. But never ever feel like you have to parent alone. We're all imperfect at this. Single parents aren't the only ones parenting alone in the physical sense. I know my husband and I endured our fair share of military deployments that left me alone at home for weeks on end. He returned to being a commercial pilot in the girls' junior high and high school years and spent many days away from the house. This is the same for many of our friends whose spouses are not only pilots, but many who are in the oil business, or other industry requiring a lot of travel, likewise leaving one parent at home alone with the kids for long periods, even years, at a time. Whatever your situation (*and especially if you're a single parent*), don't do this by yourself. And having said all of that, with regard to single parents, you may indeed not only be parenting alone in the physical sense but also in the emotional sense. That is surely something I have *not* had to deal with in spite of many separations brought on by my husband's career. Again, don't do this by yourself physically or emotionally. Find someone to step into that gap for you and do so for both your and your child's sake. We cannot do it all alone! We were never wired that way.

Over the years I have had more than one person mentor me who is in a different parenting season than I. Paul and I often reminisce about the different conversations we have had with so many different people who loved us enough to speak into our lives about the huge job before us, growing human beings into adults. It is a lofty assignment for any of us, how much more so if we were trying to do it alone? Asking for help is not a sign of weakness. On the contrary, it is a sign of strength. Furthermore, it just proves how much you love and care for your child when you reach out to others for emotional support and parenting advice in times of both stress and joy.

In the course of my marriage, physical separation has caused me to have to do lots of "stuff" on my own that I would have rather not done at all, such as doing handyman jobs around the house, or dealing with sundry other repair people and any and every household chore known to mankind. That separation also left me alone for long hours, the long days turning into long nights taking care of our children alone. But one thing for which I am ever grateful I have not had to do alone, in spite of that separation, is parent alone emotionally. That's no good. No matter who you are. No matter your personal circumstances. Find someone or somebody to come along beside you and support you in this ginormous emotional undertaking of raising a child.

RESIST THE URGE TO LIVE VICARIOUSLY THROUGH YOUR CHILD

Just because you were prom queen doesn't mean they have to be, or want to be. If you had told me years ago, "Judy, one day you will have a daughter on the drill team," I would have said, "No way!" But hey, I got a sweet little gal who did just that beautifully. I never saw that coming. Paul would love for someone to be a pilot. I would expect one out of three might follow my footsteps into law enforcement. So far no takers. At any rate, let them own their own thing. Don't push them into something that is really all about YOU, and not a single thing about them. And while it's so necessary for us to be wise guides, try not to put the kibosh on their dream just because it's not yours! This is especially difficult when they are going to college on your dime. Our daughter chose to major in theatre. We had different ideas on what she should major in, of course. But she had her heart set on theatre. In the end, we wanted her to "own" her decision, and see it to the end, whatever that end might be.

There are clear advantages to that for us parents. We preserve our relationship down the road when they either succeed or experience setbacks or failures in their chosen vocation. For our daughter, college was (and is) a new beginning. Our expectation is for all of our girls to be eventually on their own and supporting themselves financially. *They know this.* That being understood at the onset, we stepped sideways and let Shelby make her own decision about her college major. She is nearly ready to graduate now and has blown us away with what she has accomplished and how carefully and thoughtfully she is planning her future.

I fully understand that your personal resources and finances may require you to influence their choices of a college and a college major, more or less depending on your situation. Absolutely! My point is this: include them in all of the steps along the way. Listen to their input. For instance, if it's necessary that they attend only a state school, then at least give them some choices of schools. They may not want to follow the exact educational plan you have had outlined for them since they came out of the womb. This should not come as a surprise if you raised kids to think for themselves. Be open to what they have to say. Listen for cues. Just because they have a different idea about their future from what you had planned doesn't mean theirs is a bad idea. The more input they have in this decision that ultimately affects *them* for the rest of *their* lives, the less chance you have of ostracizing them from you and causing them to shut down emotionally. Keep the lines of communication open when it comes to their choices of extracurricular activities in elementary, junior high and high school, and also when it comes to choices of colleges and majors. You might be heartily and pleasantly surprised at the great things that result from decisions based on more of a collaborative approach as opposed to decisions made unilaterally by you, the parent.

BE LIFETIME LEARNERS, ALWAYS OPEN FOR CORRECTION

When Shelby was little, and I was "verbally lighting into her" while at our friend's house, my friend Susan said to me "Well, you are hard on her!" What? Me? Hard on her? Well…okay, sure, I've been overbearing with my kids since then, but I took that admonishment to heart and never forgot it. I since have tried to separate (with multiple failures) my emotions from rational thinking. It's hard. Surround yourself with friends and family members like mine who tell you the truth, not just what makes you feel good about yourself.

Furthermore, we live in an age of information. This can be information overload, but nevertheless, it leaves us without excuse in terms of our ability to be lifetime learners. We should be mature and grown up enough to have the courage to test our traditions and beliefs against quality resources that have integrity and are factually based.

I knew a story once about a woman who bought a twenty-pound ham for Christmas every year and hacked off a huge end of it prior to baking. One day her friend asked her why. She said, "It's how my grandmother cooked it, and it always turns out delicious." So she believed, apparently, there was something that needed trimmed from the ham in order to render all of that good taste. This made sense. After all, her grandmother always hacked off the end of it before baking. Nevertheless, her friend's curiosity led her to inquire as to her grandmother's intention. Alas, she asked her one day, "Grandma, why do you always hack off one end of the ham before baking it?" Grandma said, "So it would fit in my pan." So now this woman realized that for a number of years, she had been wasting a good portion of perfectly edible ham and money based on something that had become tradition. Grounded in what? A misconception. A misunderstanding. She didn't even know for sure.

This is a funny (and true) story. But we do the same things with old wives' tales, family traditions, antiquated and outdated information, internet articles that aren't grounded in research, and just being set in our ways. It wouldn't do us any good to not keep up with the updates on our computers and our phones. We can, but eventually it goes south, and the device no longer works the way it is supposed to work. Updates make your operating system on your computer work with maximum benefit and efficiency. It's the same way for information that we consume. When we continue to learn, this maximizes our ability to parent effectively. It doesn't mean we are always wrong. Of course not. But we can often be wrong, dead wrong, and yet stubbornly continue to struggle down that parenting path when we could have easily enjoyed a much smoother ride if only we had been more open to learning and accepting constructive correction. Furthermore, our unwillingness to give credence to credible resources and information that is full of integrity, can also put our child's health (and other children) at risk, both their emotional and physical health.

QUIT BUYING THEM EVERYTHING

When we were really young, married with no kids, my sister Cindy gave me some great advice about raising kids. She said, "One of the hardest things will be for you and Paul *NOT* to buy them things just because you can! Then, Judy, what do you get for them when they are sixteen? Or eighteen? *Nothing is special.*" That's one of the reasons I have always tried to save expensive items for special occasions. Our kids have everything they need; they don't need something as soon as it hits the store shelves. And it's hard enough living in the "land of plenty" (as we most certainly do here in America) to teach them gratitude and compassion. To this I say, "Just say no!" You can do it. All three of our daughters saved up their money for their own laptops. They were purchased around Christmastime because we agreed on supplying the last bit of money as a Christmas gift. They learned a lot about finances, what it means to save up for something, and moreover, they really value their possession since they were personally responsible for saving the money that purchased it. And when they lose it or break it—yes, sir, they replace it. Or *WE* replace it at a special occasion such as Christmas or birthday. "Any day that you break or lose something" does not equal a special-occasion day.

Discipline Isn't Optional

Even though we live in a culture that has evolved from being a parent to being a "buddy," discipline is not optional, people. It's not so much about outcomes as it is your example of action and follow through. Remember this: your decision to discipline is not contingent upon their past or present responses to your disciplinarian action. We do it because it's the right thing to do. It sets up expectations for the rest of their lives. Sometimes the responses we desire are seen much later. It's like continuing to offer them veggies whether they eat them or not. We know what healthy eating looks like and what it does not look like. Just as we know what healthy behavior looks like and what it's not. So just as we value physical health in our family, so we value healthy behavior. Therefore, we value discipline. It should not be easily discarded or carelessly disregarded by the parent. It's paramount. Does that include spanking? I don't know. If I had to do it all over again, I would not spank. But as parents we have to make those decisions. The rule of thumb with spanking is that "it better never be done out of anger." You must be honest with yourself. How often do you spank out of frustration and anger rather than intentional, thought out, planned, and calm?

Whatever your preconceived notions about discipline, the important thing to take away from this tip: don't throw discipline along the wayside. Kids need to understand that there are consequences for their behavior, both right and wrong. What is the most important point about discipline? <u>Doing it *and* follow through</u>. If you say to your child, "If you throw a fit in the store today, we are not going to the county fair," but then they do throw a fit in the store and you *STILL* take them to the county fair; that is reckless. You cannot be trusted to keep your word, and your child knows to disregard not only the discipline that you threaten to dole out but also promises, instruction, or guidance on any matter. I'll say it again. Discipline is paramount. Get with your parenting partner on this matter. Take a united front with your spouse or parenting partner. It is in their best interest.

APATHY OR WORRY?
BOTH ARE LETHAL WEAPONS TO
EFFECTIVE PARENTING

D on't ever say, "Well, I did it, so they're going to do it anyway." This one really requires no explanation. It reeks of ignorance. Did you have sex when you were fifteen? Did you drink and become drunk in your teens or twenties? Ever drive drunk? Were you (are you) addicted to pornography, narcotics, or prescription drugs? Did you disrespect your parents and teachers? Did you steal something? What regretful behavior from your past have you laid upon the back of your child? To what inevitable black pit in life have you assigned them because, after all, "I did that, too, and a tiger can't change his stripes"? Use your experiences as a teaching tool. Use them as reminders to love and cherish your children enough to gently lead them along a different path. It can happen. We can make a different decision about the future we want for our children minus the personal baggage of shame, guilt, or apathy rendered by our own past. I am definitely proof of that. Be sure and read Tip #50: No One Gets a Free Pass!

The polar opposite of apathetic parenting is "consumed with worry," over controlling parenting. If we are consumed with worry, we have a tendency to want to control everything. It is difficult to make lucid decisions. Inevitably, our decisions are driven more by a sense of irrational fear than they are driven by sound judgement. This irrational fear can include: "He can never make it on his own; they can't function without me; their mistakes will undo them." And as you can guess, this list spawned by worry can be endless.

Both apathy (hands off) and worry (hands on) can be detrimental to raising positive and capable children. Be wary of either extreme and find your middle ground. This isn't about compromise. It is about using our past experiences and our present circumstances to parent our kids to become positive, whole, and capable adults.

PLEASE DON'T LIE TO YOUR KIDS

Sure, this seems like a no-brainer. But you would be surprised. Lying to your kids when they ask you a direct question is setting them up for the land of poor choices, self-destruction, and estrangement. Little lies or big lies. Or intentionally omitting the truth. Don't fall into that trap. You may be forfeiting your relationship with your child in the long run in exchange for self-satisfaction in the short run. But that satisfaction will be short lived. Eventually they will know the truth, and when they do, all bets are off. Your "good intentions" will be trumped by the lies and the omissions of truth that accompanied the original discussion. When I discussed abstinence and other choices about sex with my girls, you can bet they asked if I was a virgin when I got married. "No!" was the quick, truthful answer. It set the stage for an open and honest dialogue about the consequences that choice had for me, as well as the implications of their own choices (Tip #25). If you come from a family of liars (or a "nonconfrontational, passive-aggressive, always avoid the issues" kind of family), stop that cycle of dysfunction right now! This does NOT mean sharing truths with your kids that are either 1) totally unnecessary or 2) age inappropriate! Not. At. All. But being honest with your spouse and your children (taking into consideration your child's age at the time of the discussion) will largely determine their ability to make constructive decisions and also to be fully honest and successful in committed relationships as both teens and adults.

This is a short and sweet tip. There's not a lot more to say. If you have a habit of lying to your kids because you think telling them Santa Claus is at your house will enable them to leave the party without throwing a fit, or else you omit the truth when they ask about your alcohol use as a teenager or you let them live in that delusional world where money grows on trees as you rack up credit card debt in order to give them all the things that you didn't have, you are on a collision course with calamity and you and your children will swallow a bitter pill. Tell the truth. Don't be a family of liars or one that regularly omits the truth to avoid conflict. Doing so, only creates more and worse conflict. More and worse consequences for you and your children.

LET THEM BE KIDS

According to a plethora of research, girls and boys are entering adolescence three times as early as they were fifty years ago, or even twenty years ago. The obvious problem with that is their emotional growth is not nearly in step with their physical growth, the latter of which is resulting from early onset puberty. To aggravate this condition, they are pummeled by a bombardment of information-cultural messages that distort and dictate their ideas and thoughts about sex, their bodies, marriage, relationships, etc. There is much research about what actually causes early onset puberty among our kids—especially the girls. Some of those findings includes obesity, diet, and medical conditions. But in addition to that, there is research that suggests stress and environment are also playing a part in this unfortunate situation.[2]

How might our culture, or we as parents, be culpable partners in pushing our children into adolescence and "adulthood" prematurely? A relentless exposure to inappropriate media, TV, movies, video games, electronic devices, and social media. All of these things can be a battering ram for young in-formidable minds. *Sadly, our children are badgered by sexual messages and adult choices at an age when they are neither physiologically nor emotionally equipped to either process such adult information or to make such adult decisions.* Furthermore, our small children are being taught at a very young age to use their left brain at the expense of their right brain. The full onslaught of social media has debilitated our abilities as parents to teach our children the importance of play, imagination, and the sheer innocence and joy of being a little kid. In an article written by Dr. Justin Coulson for the Institute for Family Studies, regarding exposing our kids to sexual and violent content in media at inappropriate ages, Dr. Coulson cited a study by *Pediatrics Magazine* in which 1,000 parents viewed multiple violent and sexual clips, and in each one, the parent "consistently reduced their age recommendations for children as they watched more clips."[3]

> "Our digital diet is desensitizing us. The violence and sex we see is glamorized, and often consequence-free. But there *are* consequences we are not aware of. We need to wake up. By not only enduring it but embracing it — and endorsing it for our children's entertainment — we act to their detriment."

The implications of this are far-reaching and potentially dangerous. Our child's ability to interact socially, problem solve, seek conflict resolution, or just speak intelligently is seriously hampered. Let me spell this out simply. *For example*, if you have young children, they probably don't need to watch an R-rated movie or TV show, play an R-rated video game, or own a smart phone. Parents, you may indeed be the singular resounding force standing in the gap for your children between their innocence and the full onslaught of image overload that is available with just one click. They will grow up soon enough. Please while you can, let them be kids!

DON'T PRAISE THEM FOR THEIR GOOD LOOKS

It teaches them to put all their eggs into the one basket of vanity. There's nothing wrong with telling your daughter she looks beautiful in her prom dress, wedding dress, or the like. Goodness knows we are going to do that. But to always use their physical looks and their physical prowess as a selling point for how special they are, is very dicey. We ALL know that physical looks are often temporary attributes, quickly dispensable in a multitude of circumstances. Not the least of which is age! And it's just plain shallow. Character counts far more than looks. Period. Dot. It's brain over brawn (so to speak) when encouraging our children to be all they can be.

Don't Bail Them Out

When my kids were really little, we spent many hours at the park. I would cringe whenever I saw another kid take a minor fall or scrape, and the mom come swooping over and pick her up and coddle her. Over what? A scratch? The stakes are low right now, parents. Our kids definitely need to be able to live inside a safe boundary. That's the privilege we have as parents, offering our kids a safe refuge where they are unconditionally loved. However, this does not include bailing them out, coddling them, never letting them be disappointed, never making them wait for a special gift or event, or manufacturing a fake world in which they are the center of attention.

One of the **many** regretful things I did as a parent of littles is not having my kids wake up on their own with an alarm clock early on. I didn't even think about it. I just woke them up every morning. Then along about third or fourth grade, it became harder and harder to get them out of bed. I wished I had started training them to wake up on their own sooner. This is a fairly mild example of bailing out my kids. But we have *all* been guilty of answering their calls (demands) to shag something on their behalf (homework or the baseball uniform that they left at home that morning); and bringing it to them at school. Or maybe you went to the teacher and demanded to know why they couldn't retake a test. True, we are our child's biggest and best advocate. But sometimes being their advocate means *not* intervening, as often as it means intervening. Being our child's biggest advocate also means teaching them to intervene on their own behalf whenever and wherever possible. The more often we "bail them out," we potentially forfeit the golden opportunity for a great life lesson. The stakes are low NOW. One day the stakes will be higher. They'll be away from us. Someone will hurt them emotionally. They may lose a job. Do you want them to crumble or do you want them to have coping strategies for recovering from disappointment, pain, and hurt? Do you want to groom them for success in work and relationships? Quit bailing them out. Because once you start, it's an endless vicious cycle that follows you *and* them for years to come.

A few weeks ago, my middle daughter told me a story about a huge project she had completed for a college class, and after following the instructions perfectly she turned in her project. The Teacher Assistant marked off for several things that were not originally required for the assignment and gave Halle a low grade. Halle felt like this was not merited and took her case to her professor who apparently agreed with her. I was impressed with how she advocated for herself in an appropriate and professional way. Surely, she was able to do that, at least in part, because we had required her to advocate for herself wherever and whenever she could while she was still living at home with us.

Quit bailing them out. You can still be there for them when they fall. But sometimes you just have to let them fall.

DO READ WITH YOUR CHILD 💡

Reading is a gift we give to our kids. It loves them. They love it. It's about sharing ideas and having incredibly profound conversations that the book initiates for you. It is a portal to a really big world. Reading broadens their views, showing them that beyond the comfort of their small world lays a big, beautiful expanse of people, nature, and ideas just waiting for them to explore. It opens up possibilities for them. They can see themselves in successful relationships, jobs, and promising futures. You can get all that from just reading? Yes, you can. But more importantly, it is time well spent between a parent and a child. A wonderful time of love, appropriate touch, acceptance, and individual time with your child. READ. And when they are older, don't let them see the movie unless they have read the book, particularly if it is a movie based on a classic book!

If you have babies, start early. Put them on your lap. It's like one-stop shopping for parenting. You read, you love, you learn—all in one setting. Kids need to grow up knowing mom and dad value reading in order for them to value it. Some of my best toddler memories are the couch, the girls, and piles of our favorite books. Some of their most beloved memories are Paul reading chapter books to them at bedtime. READ. It's free.

It's magnificent. As teenagers, all three of our daughters created their own book lists. Since we had set the reading precedent early on in their lives, once they were teenagers, I found books I wanted them to read, and I inserted them into their own personal lists. *Yes, I had required reading.* I wanted them to appreciate their upbringing and the functionality of the home they live in, so I required *The Glass Castle* by Jeannette Walls. I wanted to make sure they had a handle on why they live in a country where they are so free. I wanted them to know something about the Americans who sacrificed everything so that they could now live in freedom. Therefore, I had them read *Unbroken* by Laura Hillenbrand. I wanted them to understand the love and grace of God and how that usurps the love of a man for them. Therefore, I had them read *Redeeming Love* by Francine Rivers. I wanted them to understand the trials and obstacles of women, young girls their own age who live in the war-torn areas of the Middle East, so I put *Infidel by* Ayaan Hirsi Ali on their reading list.

Since they are all young adults now, I have *suggested* reading additions to their lists. Often, they are more than happy to comply. Some of the sweetest words my daughter Halle ever said to me was during her senior year in high school as she was reading *The Poisonwood Bible,* by Barbara Kingsolver, for her English Literature class: "Mom, you have to read this book. You will love it." The best part of that was reading the book, and then discussing the content with Halle. What pure joy. And indeed, the book list goes on and on. Books at every single age and every single stage teach our children valuable life lessons without us even lifting a finger.

Do Choose Your Battles Wisely

"Don't die on that hill." That is a phrase (at least for me) coined by my wise sister Cindy. On more than one occasion, she warned me, "Judy, is that the hill you want to die on? Because if it is, charge! But if it's not, then find a way down." You know the one. The one that doesn't have any specific, identifiable outcome on who they are destined to become. For me, this was about my girls being allowed to wear bikini swimsuits when they were seventeen, fifteen, and fourteen, respectively. With the exception of a few modest two pieces, up to this point, I had always required my girls to wear either one piece or two pieces that had great coverage. You know what I mean. Well, about the time we moved back to the states from Germany, as the girls were really transitioning into middle school and high school years, all three of them (literally) came to me and gave me a well-thought-out appeal on the swimsuit issue. *All three of them!* I really had to think about this hard-and-fast rule that I had pretty much enforced all the years leading up to now! Again, my sister's advice rang out. Is this a battle worth fighting? The answer, I glumly admitted to myself, was a resounding "no." Maybe at one time, at one season of our life, it was, but no longer now. But that did not mean that it was no-holds-barred, anything goes. Yes, they could now purchase bikinis. But even so, there could *possibly* be a bikini out there in bikini shopping land that I would absolutely veto if necessary. It's true that even among bikinis, not all are created equal. Then also, they had to have my approval of any picture they wished to post on social media of them wearing said bikini. That was a rule that required working out some kinks. And finally, I told them that there were places where I knew the homeowners would not be comfortable with them prancing around in bikinis. In that case, they would respect the friends we were visiting and would wear shirts over their swimsuits.

One of the most common senseless battles I see parents of small children fighting is the food battle. Here was the simplest way of solving that problem. "Son, if you don't eat dinner, you don't eat dessert." Sure, some kids won't care about the prospect of losing dessert. But that's okay. The key is this: if you want them to eat their dinner (their veggies and proteins), then certainly don't reward them for *not* doing it by letting them have their treats. While it is an age-old conundrum trying to figure out how to convince kids to eat what they need to eat in order to get all the recommended nutrients, it is *not* difficult At. All. to understand that you should *not* reward them *when they don't.* They won't starve. And even if they don't eat, make them stay at the dinner table with their family. Remember, don't fight the battle of food. Just don't reward noncompliance. <u>Quit arguing about the former and stand your ground on the latter.</u>

And another common "battle" I see parents of young kids fighting is the coat-or-jacket battle. I knew parents who would argue with their kids about going outside in forty-degree weather with no coat. When they get cold, they will either come in to get warm or they will put on a coat. Yes, it's true. It's one thing if they are compromised physically with a pre-existing medical condition or an abnormality that is aggravated by changes in temperatures, wind, or rain. But otherwise, our concerns about them just getting cold isn't really enough for us to battle the coat-and-jacket war.

No, we don't want our kids to get hypothermia. But that is rarely the case in our backyards or on the playground. Let it go.

So yeah, I relented on my swimsuit rule that was age old in our family. But I also earned a lot of credibility and respect from my kids for choosing to let something go that I knew good and well was not worth the effort, or the loss of ground that it might surely bring about if I were to stand and fight. *Then* when I really do need to stand my ground on a particular issue, I find they are much less likely to respond with rebellion.

PARENTING TIP #13:

Do Be Mindful of Their Diets

Truth. Whether we want to hear it or not. There is simply so much trustworthy and reliable information available regarding nutrition for children and adults that we are virtually without excuse when it comes to understanding the dangers of too much sugar, for instance. There is always a plethora of propaganda available to us, as well. But trustworthy sources exist, like our own pediatricians and the American Academy of Pediatrics, or a number of other great online sources that are unbiased and impartial in terms of informing us what is good and what is not good to put into our mouths. Not to mention, the moms and dads who have gone before us in this parenting journey and might be able to give you solid advice or recommendations grounded in experience. I have always been a fan of cooking and baking. I still am. I will always continue to make homemade favorites that our family loves. But I have appreciated the onslaught of quality information available to me over the years regarding the risks of consuming the wrong kinds of fats, or the risks of consuming an overabundance of sugar. I am not a nutritionist and perhaps neither are you, right? So we *should and can* be aware of current nutritional science that serves to keep our families healthy. It is in this vein that I offer you a few tips that helped us along the way.

First, keep giving them veggies: never allow yourself to fall into that trap of "He just does not like green beans or spinach and won't eat them, therefore I'm just not going to offer them to him any longer." My kids changed so much throughout the years with regard to their likes and dislikes when it came to food. I think the key was this: we always put it on their plate, even in small bites. And generally speaking, we all ate the same food prepared at the same meal, until they were quite old enough to articulate truly what they liked and did not like. Until a certain point in their growth and maturation, their dislikes had as much to do with aesthetics and textures (looks and feel) as it did actual taste. That is the big argument for continuing to offer our littles nutritional food items, even though they won't eat it at the given moment. Moment of confession: as young adults, I have two out of three now who eat a plethora of vegetables and a variety of foods. My youngest is not a good vegetable eater. I lament this often. And if I were completely honest, I probably let down on my "job" in this area when she was a toddler and forward. She was my youngest, and while some things get easier to do with multiples, other things get tiresome. Nevertheless, it is never too late. We still advocate a healthy diet for her and try to be creative in encouraging her in ways to improve. (She won't eat zucchini alone, but she loves it in bean burritos.) Bottom line is, remember Tip #12 when choosing your battles. Don't fight the food battle so much as stick to the "no sweets rule when you don't eat your meal first." And keep offering them the good stuff. Even if you can't force them to eat it (no, we can't), what you *can* control is refined sugar. You have the ability to totally limit how much of this they get in their diets. You don't have to look very far to see all of the havoc diets high in refined sugar are reeking in our lives. Truly this is one of those "we live in an age of information" issues. That being the case, we have no excuse for allowing our kids to indulge in an overabundance of sugar and junk food, fast food included, and soda, while putting their health at risk in the process.

Teach Them Life Skills: Tips #14–18

Teach Them how to Ride a Bike

When we lived in Germany, we moved there with an eight-, nine-, and eleven-year-old. All three of them already knew how to ride a bike. And boy oh boy, were we happy for that because unbeknownst to us, we discovered our new home in Germany had literally hundreds of miles of intersecting farm roads, actually starting right out of our front door. We could bike to coffee shops, restaurants, and markets. When we moved, both Halle and Katie Ann said they would miss the bike riding more than anything else, and they had tears in their eyes when they said it. Bike riding was so prolific in Germany that it was like leaving an old friend behind when we moved to heavily populated Houston, Texas, not known for being a bike-friendly city. Bike riding is a fun, exciting, family activity no matter where you live. And virtually every town in which we have ever lived, the kids in the neighborhoods are often out playing together with scooters, and bicycles. Teach them to ride a bike. It could even save them a lot of embarrassment as they get older. For instance, if they are the only one in their friend group who cannot ride a bike, or if they are unable to participate in a bike tour, or heaven forbid if they ever have to turn down an invitation from a group of friends as an adult, or a date because she never learned how to ride a bike, it could be an awkward and sad situation for your kiddo. It's sometimes the little things in life that bring us so much joy. Bike riding is one of those things for me and has always been so for our family. During our tour in Germany, we participated in bike tours in several European cities. Absolutely some of our favorite memories were made with *Fat Tire Bike Tours* in four different countries. Your child's biking experience may very well happen primarily in your neighborhood, but don't deprive them of this precious skill and hallmark pleasure of their childhood.

PARENTING TIP #15:

Teach Them How to Swim

When I was not quite six years old, my parents drowned senselessly in a fishing accident. I say senselessly because my father did not really know how to swim. He panicked, started slapping at water rather than using his hands to swim or paddle, and in the end, both he and my mother succumbed. They literally could have dog paddled out of that pond. We were at a swim party one evening many years ago, when our three girls were quite young. Halle (eight years old at the time) went flying off the diving board into the deep end before we could say "carrot soup." I was literally one second from jumping in. Because we were *with* her, we felt she was never in danger of drowning. In fact, there was no real panic on our part, just a quick brisk decision to get in the water with her. But before I could even do that, her sister Shelby, who was just ten years old, swam over to Halle's position, went under water, and just pushed Halle to the surface. Shelby already knew not only how to swim, but how to react (to our utter surprise) in a swimming pool situation, where she spied another child (in this case her sister) clearly out of her league in the deep end of the pool. We were shocked and awed. Shelby pushed Halle to the edge of the pool, and we scooped her up and out. Then as easily and effortlessly as she had rescued her sister from the deep end, she turned and swam away to the other side of the pool. None of our girls were swim team material. They never showed an interest in organized swimming, and really that was not their skill set. But indeed, they all three *know how to swim.* I was in "Mommy and Me" swim classes with them before they could walk. Red Cross classes at the local university in the summer, or the YMCA indoor pool in the winter. By the time they were three years old, they were in classes with their instructors alone without a parent. Would knowing how to swim save their life? Maybe it would and maybe it would not. It truly depends on the circumstance and how much peril surrounds those circumstances in any given situation. But on the other hand, if your child does *not* know how to swim, then you can answer in the affirmative that they will for sure *not* have that option, if indeed the time comes when they are unexpectedly faced with a situation where their life may require it. And I know personally what a travesty that can be. It would have been so easy for me, given the loss I experienced with my parents, to keep my kids *out* of the water. But I am so thankful that did not happen. My husband and I both enjoy water activities and water sports. And had we eliminated biking and swimming from the list, there would have been so many absolutely wonderful family experiences, vacations, and traditions that would never have happened over the years. Memories and photographs by the scores that simply would not exist. As it is, our kids can swim, and our kids can ride a bike. And they will gladly pass on those traditions to their own children.

TEACH THEM HOW TO
DRIVE A STICK SHIFT

On my way home from college for Christmas break 1983, I had a wreck. I totaled my 1974 Chevrolet Wagon (adorned with wood panels—I just added this little tidbit for fun!). Fortunately, I had only paid $400.00 for said vehicle. Unfortunately, I now needed a car. I grew up in Indiana where in the winter and at Christmas (especially in the 80s), you could always expect lots of snow. Well, it happened that this Christmas break, there was quite a bit of snow on the ground. Yes, snow was piled up everywhere when I purchased my 1976 Honda Civic four-speed manual, straight stick on the floor! I'm only sorry I no longer have any pictures of my old car. And in the dead of winter, on icy, snowy roads, my boyfriend at the time graciously taught me how to drive a stick shift. I would have bought an automatic, but after a thorough search, this car was all I could afford. I did pull it off. And the next three cars I purchased all had a manual transmission. When I was working for the Drug Enforcement Administration (DEA) years later, I found, as a requirement in my job, that I was continually jumping into different cars for different sundry reasons, and oftentimes they were stick shift. I was expected to know how to drive one. I can't tell you how embarrassing that would've been had I been called on to admit to all "the guys" that I did not know how to drive a manual transmission. Ugh. When we moved to Europe, on many different occasions we had to rent a car. We would pick up the rental car and discover it was a stick shift. It came to our attention that had we wanted an automatic, we would've had to make a special request for that. And it would be so much more expensive.

My oldest daughter was my first to learn how to drive a manual transmission. She was quite angry at me and insisted she did not understand the necessity. Katie Ann, our youngest, was the second to learn. Halle, our middle daughter, was the last to learn. Katie Ann took it mostly in stride and was pretty reticent about learning. Now she brags unabashedly to her platonic boy friends at school that she has deftly acquired this little skill, and well…they have not. The other two fought it, but I stood my ground. Unfortunately for them, back in the day, their mother was an eighteen-year-old girl who needed a car to get back to school more than she needed the comfort of an automatic. And there was no one buying a car *for* her. So fast-forward back to the McCarver clan. We agreed to buy all of them at least one car for certain. We agreed that car would be inexpensive, but dependable and functional. It would be a stick shift. They conceded. Undoubtedly, this is entirely a parenting tip of the "optional" variety, (unlike, for instance, Tips #19 or #37). *BUT* if you're looking for ways to increase your child's self-confidence, or ways to make them "stretch" themselves outside their comfort zones, this is a great tip! And as an additional bonus, it's much harder to text, eat, or make phone calls while driving a stick shift! And very rarely does anyone ask to borrow it. There's that.

Teach Them How to Cook and Do Household Cleaning Chores

Still, even after years of parenting and hanging out with friends, I am constantly amazed at how many of our friends, and parents in general, do not require their children to help with the dishes, cook meals, or clean the house. ❡ We started early with our girls. When they were two years old they were helping to take dishes to the sink and also picking up their toys. Being a part of a family means also being a part of a team. They are already so privileged to live inside a warm house in winter, or a cool house in the summer. And while we are on that subject, they also have indoor plumbing. They can surely learn to do some dishes and how to wash clothes. When we have dinner company, our girls get up from the table without being asked, and they clear the dishes. They didn't always do it without being asked. We insisted. Now they do so without being asked. And it's glorious and precious. It's not unusual for our company to stare with open mouths in disbelief. Then the girls also clean the kitchen and bring in desert to our company. They do this not only because it is expected of them but also to honor us, their parents. But whatever the reason, it's very nice. And I love it.

Our kids can also make their way around the kitchen. Halle loves to cook. Katie loves to bake. Shelby loves to eat. Shelby will indeed do whatever necessary to get a meal at a restaurant if no one else at home is cooking. But all of them know how to cook *something*. This is not just a way of domesticating your children. And this is not just for daughters. This is for sons, too. It is a way for both boys and girls to learn to take care of themselves, and who knows? It could also be a way for them to gift someone they care about with homemade food or a dessert, which they themselves created. We have endured all of the typical mishaps you would expect from kids working in the kitchen. This includes spilled milk, burnt bread, burnt cookies, and Shelby texting us when we were out to town to show us a picture of 1.5 pounds of frozen hamburger sitting in a skillet with the question, "Should I have thawed this first?" She was making tacos. But if Tips #21 and #22 happen as we hope they will, then it is so important that she knows how to navigate and negotiate a kitchen. They don't have to leave home as semi-professional chefs or anything. But certainly, they should have some basic recipes in their repertoire.

If your children cannot find their way around the stove or refrigerator without scratching their heads, consider helping them by giving them a few simple lessons and working together on a few basic dishes. It's not only a great life skill, but it's such a fun and loving way to spend time together.

It's so much easier as parents to do all of the household chores and all of the cooking. I, too, have been guilty of not discharging enough duties to my overprivileged children. One of the sweetest (and most triumphant) things ever said to me by one of my children was by Shelby in her first year in college: "Mom, I did not realize how much you did for me." It's true that in the time it takes for us to convince our kids they have to do the task, and then show them how to do it, we could've completed the job three or four times over. This is especially true if you're a type A personality like me. ❡ But it's absolutely paramount we charge them with picking up toys, cleaning their rooms and bathrooms, working in the yard, and helping in the kitchen. And we elected *not* to pay them for completing these basic chores. It shows honor and respect to not only their parents, but to all other family members while teaching life skills all at the same time. We shouldn't rob our kids of these grand learning opportunities by doing everything ourselves either because it is easier and more convenient, or because we just don't want to make our children responsible. Include them!

TEACH THEM THE ART OF HANDWRITTEN NOTES

When I was a little girl, my grandmother wrote in her journal every single day. She also sent handwritten Christmas cards and letters. She was a writer in every sense of the word. Not one of those words were published, but still, she was a prolific and avid writer. I learned a lot from her when it came to the power of the pen. I took that into adulthood, and always tried to be thankful with a handwritten note. Don't just think about it. Do it. If you really appreciated something someone did for you, then write it down for them. This is a powerful relationship tool. And it has a ripple effect for years to come.

What I did not realize back when I was a young girl, what I could not foresee, was how social networking would one day virtually replace the handwritten note. First it was emails, and now of course it is every imaginable social networking electronic feed conceivable, which has virtually replaced any thought we once had of putting pen to paper. In fact, in some cases, it has even *replaced our thoughts*. Truly, social networking posts and messages are at times so thoughtless and meaningless. After all, I think there is an emoji for virtually every emotion under the sun. When our girls were toddlers and could not write yet, we had them scribble a picture and their name on a card (unintelligible scribbles) for a friend who had a birthday or a sympathy card for someone who lost a loved one. As they grew older, we made them handwrite thank-you notes for birthday gifts. We also required them to write a note of gratitude to a friend who had done something very special for them. If they preferred to draw, that was perfectly acceptable. And I had veto power. If I felt like that note was perfunctory and without any real emotion, only done to satisfy a parental requirement, I would tell them to think about it for a while and rewrite it later. The draft then went into the trash. Training happens everywhere in parenting. Even how to handwrite notes with authenticity. We can teach them what is acceptable and not acceptable. For instance, you can actually teach your son or daughter that it is unacceptable to break up with their significant other over Instagram. You can require them to write thank-you notes when people give them a gift. You can and should require them to dig down deep to expose true and authentic emotions when it comes to expressing their sympathy, joy, or gratitude in a handwritten note.

THE PARENT TRAP:
TIPS #19-20

PARENTING TIP #19:

Don't Be a Child-Centered Family

We spend a lot of time and ink in this book discussing why we should be great parents to our kids. It might appear at the outset that we are suggesting to you that "it's all about the kids." That couldn't be farther from the truth. Actually, it's exactly the opposite of what I am proposing. If you go through each of these tips, you'll find that while it's true many of them are intended to draw you together as a family, even so, the majority of them inherently draws your child out of the center of the spotlight. For instance, Serving Others (Tip #24), and Encouraging Sibling Relationships (Tip #46); all of these create a sense of humility in our children and set them on a journey of "doing" rather than "getting." All of these tips foster in our child a sensitivity to other people's pain or plight in life. This book is intended *to help you help your child* know how to look outward at the needs of others, not constantly inward. If we are doing what we need to be doing as parents, for instance in Tips #11, 31, and 47, then hopefully, their self-esteem and sense of self-worth and confidence should be amply covered, without the need of falling into the trap of raising them to be child-centered, and so every thought in their heads that goes in and comes out is about their own personal comfort.

What are the risks of a being a child-centered family? And what does that look like exactly? Well, first of all, it is not exact. As parents we may be too child centered in just one particular area—like always allowing the child to determine where we eat dinner. Because, after all, little Susie only eats cheese pizza, so she simply cannot be accommodated by any other restaurant that sells meat or vegetables—or, *stop the press*, doesn't sell pizza at all. Other parents can be child centered in pretty much every area of their lives. How they vacation, where they vacation; whether or not they go out on Friday night EVER again without their child, whether or not they are willing to leave them with a trusted babysitter, who's in charge at home (parent or child), and who makes the final decisions in their house. If you are not able to have people over to your house, or join a church, or do anything socially, because your children go to bed too early; or if you are paralyzed with fear that their routine might be upset, or they might embarrass us in public situations or in our home with guests, then you may well be living in a child-centered home.

My husband and I had our share of epic fails on many occasions as parents, but one thing for sure that we took great pains to avoid was this notion of raising child-centered kids. In fact, as the girls were growing up, when they disagreed in force with a decision one of us made, he would tell them, "This family is not a democracy." He would remind them that indeed, "You get input, but final decisions do not come to a vote around here. Your mom and I have both veto power *and* the final say." (We might have voted on things like restaurant choices, but the big stuff, nope!) You may say that was more of a dictatorship. We truly gave them age-appropriate choices through each stage of their young lives. That's so important if we want them to be prepared to make choices for themselves later. For all the rest, we insisted on being the parent. Credibility helped us. What do I mean by that? Well, by making sure that we had all pistons firing in other areas and with other important Tips, such as #5, 7, and 12.

❢ If your child usurps your marriage relationship, you are in a child-centered home. If that child does not respect one of his parents, and the other parent does nothing to stop that disrespect, you are sending the message to your son or daughter that your spouse is not worthy of respect, and certainly that your son or daughter is more important to you than your spouse.

Moreover, I have always valued date nights with my husband, knowing that one of these days, it will revert back to being just he and I, which indeed it has. I want to preserve and protect our relationship together. If our kids always take the number one spot in our lives, and we relegate one another to number two, the marriage will suffer and perhaps irrevocably so.

Along these lines we must, as much as possible, always take a united front in front of our kids. I want to insert an exception clause right here and right now. If your spouse is abusing you or your child, you cannot, either morally or legally, take a united front with them. Children cannot advocate for themselves in these situations. If you have a spouse who is physically or sexually abusing a child in his care, and you stand by and do nothing, shame on you. You have effectively rendered that child without hope and without an advocate. But thankfully, for the majority of us, this is not the case. So indeed, you need to quit deferring to your child's wishes and take a united front with your spouse. If you don't, you undermine your spouse's parenting role and their ability to influence your child. It's demeaning and disrespectful. Does this mean we agree with everything our spouse does? No, it most certainly does not. There were many cases where Paul and I deferred to one another due to time constraints, work schedules, or temperament. Shelby's first year of college was accompanied by a typical amount of anxiety for her. There were multiple times when I was happy to defer a text message or a phone call to her dad to give me a mental break and to allow him to offer her new insights and encouragement when I felt like I was at the short end of my stick. I did most of the driving instruction. My temperament fared a little better than Paul's in this situation. (Ask our girls!) Furthermore, in the interest of communication and open dialogue with your spouse (or the ex-spouse), you two should be discussing the health and welfare of your child or children together. Therefore, if the two of you disagree, it's on both of you to work out some sort of a compromise when it comes to the decision at hand. Your children don't need to believe that you agree on everything. They just need to know that you are going to take a united front when it comes to big decisions. There's a big difference between the two agreeing on everything and the two taking a united front. We do the same with our teachers and people in authority. I didn't always agree with everything a teacher did, how they graded, or their teaching methods. If I absolutely had to, I held a conference. But in the end, you can bet I never allowed our kids to usurp the teacher's authority or be disrespectful. If they did, there were consequences. It's simply reckless parenting when you don't back each other up. If your children are told "no" by one parent, but they know they can always get what they want conversely from the other parent, then you're most definitely living in a child-centered home. Our kids are smart, and they will exploit that gap between the two of you, and blow everything and everyone up in the process.

Child-centered homes at any age make the child's choices and their desires, whims, complaints, joy, and wants the number one priority of the home at the expense of what is for their very best.

For years our girls were babysitters. They were (still are) loving and seasoned babysitters. We have some acquaintances who have one child and needed a sitter for only about three hours in the evening in their home. It was a school night for him and for my daughter. When my daughter said, "No problem, but I'll need to bring my homework," the mom immediately quipped up, "No, that will not work." Apparently, her six-year-old son would require my daughter's undivided attention while he was watching TV or playing with Legos. As a result, our daughter was never asked to babysit for them again. My kids are very attentive sitters. I have always taught them "Baby/Child first." Because of this, they get down on the floor with them and engage them, feed them, love on them. But in this case, it was clearly a school night and for only a couple of hours, and by the parent's own admission, he would just be playing Legos or watching television. And yet, whatever event those parents had to sacrifice that evening apparently paled in comparison to the concern of having a babysitter doing her homework in the same room while their child watched television.

Take your child out of the center spotlight. Do not make her the center of attention. If you do, she will most certainly demand it again and again and again. If you raise your children in such a way that they take precedence over even the smallest issues and facets of your family life, then it will always be about them. They will go out into that cold, real world demanding the same treatment they are used to getting at home, and the results could be devastating when they realize that is not how the real world is at all. If indeed you continually protect them from disappointment, minimize losing and magnify winning, emphasize their looks with perpetual praise, and downplay the importance of character, you may indeed be a child-centered family.

PARENTS, THE WORLD DOESN'T REVOLVE AROUND US EITHER

S elflessness in parenting. What does that look like? Parenting is inherently sacrificial. That's just the way it is. Welcome to this life we chose the very minute we *chose* to get involved in such activities that produce children. We may not be able to golf every weekend or party with our gal pals like we're still single (because *I'm* not). We may have to cancel a party if our baby has a 103-degree fever. We may have to go to an amusement park for fun (*their* fun) or a library or a bookstore or a Lego store. We may need to stomp in rain puddles with the rain pouring down while our child joyfully stomps along beside us. We may have to postpone a hobby because their extracurricular activity is prioritized over ours, and both cannot fit in the family budget. Tip #19 reminds us it's not all about our kids. But this tip necessarily reminds us that it's not all about us, either. When we lived in Europe for four years, one of my favorite things to do in virtually every city we visited was to climb the belfry of the cathedral or whatever steps could be found in that city. And they were everywhere! Beautiful, majestic, and looming over the city, I wanted to see those views from the top of every single belfry we encountered. I cannot tell you how many belfries I dragged my kids up and down. I did that because *I wanted to* and because life is not all about them. The world doesn't revolve around them. They needed to understand this important principle if they are to learn unselfishness. But during the time we lived in Europe, we also went to about four different amusement parks, including Euro Disney. (We've still never been to Stateside Disneyland as a family!) Several times we took their friends with us. I went to indoor water parks, petting zoos, and a number of other places of their choosing. We went to these "alternative attractions" not because I wanted to, but because *they wanted to*, and well…life isn't all about me, either.

We have always played board games with our girls. I can remember the early years, board games indicated appropriate ages for players on the box, for instance "eight and under." They should've included along with that "eight and under—*plus a parent.*" We played our fair share of the Matching Game, Operation, Sorry, and Candy Land—not games that required a lot of strategy, but it did require humility and a desire to be with your son or daughter. Again, we did it because *they wanted* to play the game!

The Psalmist tells us the sacrifices that God wants from us are not material. "The sacrifices of God are a broken spirit, a broken and a contrite heart—These, O God, You will not despise" (Psalm 51:17, NKJV). A broken heart was the sacrifice God wanted. In this same passage, He rejected the Israelites' burnt offerings, the very sacrifices they were commanded to make. Why would He do such a thing? He rejected them because they did not come from a heart of thankfulness or from a heart broken over their own sins. The burnt offerings were simply perfunctory in nature. They were on autopilot with their sacrifices. And God said, "No! That's not the sacrifice I want."

If the only sacrifice we make for our kids is providing for basic life needs, but we are emotionally disconnected from them, maybe it's because we've made the whole relationship secondary to our own wants and desires that are mostly unrelated to our children. In that case, our relationship with our children is transactional only, not deep and personal.

Paul and I are in that stage of life that necessitates discussions about retirement, where to live next, and all that goes along with this. Now, our girls are all away at college. Ostensibly, they will not live with us again. But while your kids are *still at home*, decisions that don't include them or decisions that push them to the edges of your life together, nudging them out, could be premature and could be damaging to your relationship. When your kids start driving themselves everywhere and are more self-sufficient, it is certainly easier (and necessary) to loosen up the reins of control. But it is also too easy for those years to slip right through your fingers because they *are* so self-sufficient and *can* drive themselves everywhere. When Katie was the last one at home, I continued to make an effort to play Skategories with her. It was not unusual for me to walk in the house and find her and Paul at the table playing a card game of Skip-Bo or perhaps playing Yatzhee with Halle if she were home on a school break. Shelby's personal favorite is Monopoly. And if Halle and I happen to be out together doing necessary errands, she usually wants to go to the coffee shop. Me being the taskmaster that I am, I usually want to either go home and get back to work or continue getting more errands done. I usually concede to the coffee. It is undiluted one-on-one time with my daughter, and it is amazing the things she tells me sitting in that coffee shop in that very moment that I choose to say, "Yes, I can do that." I know that the more often I am separated from them, caught up in my own work or personal interests, the more I am going to lose precious time with them. Your kids will be gone soon enough. And when they are, you will have a lot of time on your hands. Don't lead a child-centered life (Tip #19). Let them fly (Tip #21). But none of that means we allow our own personal and professional interests, careers, or hobbies to crowd them out completely, or to abdicate our responsibilities as engaged parents to others: grandparents, friends, schools, daycares, youth pastors. It is our charge to be engaged with our children at all stages of their growth. Only then can we expect them to be fully equipped to engage their world.

LETTING THEM GO:
TIPS #21–22

"Fly Like an Eagle..."

Let your kids go! I literally knew a young lady who was twenty-one years old and had an incredible opportunity that she declined for no other reason than she was unwilling to part from her family. She was offered an all-expense paid internship on the West Coast, 1,000 miles away from home. But she turned it down. And essentially, her stated reason is that she did not want to separate from her mother. I knew another mother who literally arranged her daughter's marriage so that she would not move away from home. (Arranged marriages are not typical of American culture.) I have known people whose decisions for where (geographically) to build their career and establish residence were based on their belief that when their children married in this particular geographical location, they would be far less likely to move away from their parents. Don't misunderstand this. I love family time. I have herein devoted numerous pages to the endorsement of same, making claims hitherto that family time should be restored and rebuilt in the American family and that it contributes to the wholeness and health of our children. We have treasured and prioritized our family time with our three girls, whether in the form of dinner around the kitchen table, or family vacations, Friday night board games, or any number of other family activities together. On the other hand, what we have *not* treasured or prioritized is "how to keep my daughter from moving away." Just the opposite. Every single day that we have had them with us has carried with it the realization that one day they could be gone, and not only gone, but perhaps far away from us. Some of this has been our teaching and expectation. But admittedly, the assumption that they are going to live apart from us has happened because we have always told them, "You can be whatever you want to be." That carries with it an inherent understanding, that "*whatever they want to be*" may also be somewhere other than near us. Moreover, because we've traveled away from home often, their exposure to the world has rendered an attitude of independence in them. I realize that not all of you have the advantage of having lived overseas and travelled extensively abroad. But most of us have the opportunity to take our children to neighboring cities, and states. Do "staycations" in your own region. It will amaze you what you find out about your own hometown or home state. History is that way. It's a relentless teacher of the past, our own past. And it is not very far from you geographically. Expose your children to as much of it as possible. And if possible, take longer trips farther away from home. First of all, it is a lot of fun, but it will also prepare and equip them for later in life, when they get the opportunity to head out on their own solo adventures without their family (Tip #45). I know people who won't send their kids to summer camp for a week and then wonder why they turn down incredible opportunities as teens and young adults. What does it take for a son or daughter to arrive at twenty-one*ish* years old and be ready to fly the coop?

When we arrived in Germany on a four-year tour at NATO, our oldest daughter Shelby turned twelve years old two weeks later. She was in the sixth grade. Precisely one year later, when she was thirteen, she had the opportunity to attend "Beach Break" in Italy with the US military services Christian youth organization. She cried and fought us over that. This would be her debut trip away from *both* her sisters and parents—the only time she separated from all of us, with the exception of occasional sleepovers with friends. We made this trip nonnegotiable. I know that seems harsh. But here were our criteria. We did it based on two very important facts. First, her dad and I were much older and wiser than her. We knew from life experience (which she decidedly lacked) that this trip would not only be fun, but it would encourage spiritual and emotional growth as well as maturity and self-confidence. And, second, we made this trip nonnegotiable because we trusted the organizer and the people whom she would accompany on the trip. We were as sure of her safety as we could possibly be. Boom! She was outvoted and outclassed by the two people who love her the most in the world—her parents. Her tears were solidly and lovingly lost on her parents' wisdom, personal life experience, and our confidence in the trip organizers.

I think as parents it sometimes makes sense to us to defer to our child's emotions in these circumstances. "Oh well, they obviously don't want to go so I'll not make them." This, in spite of the fact that in so doing, we are trusting our young child's current state of emotions at the *total disregard* of *our* life experience and wisdom. In the end, our child loses. We are simply able to see life through different lenses than our children. That is why we are the parents. Perhaps in the short run, it seems all warm and fuzzy: "Shelby doesn't want to take a beach trip to Italy with her military youth group, visit incredible sites, enjoy the beach, and forge new lasting friendships. She's happy here at home. So that's that." Everyone's happy, right? That is the short run! Now consider the long run. Shelby *did* take that trip—she was so homesick the first two days that by her own admission, she had a knot in her throat that literally prevented her from eating the first twenty-four hours. But by the third day, she had adjusted and was able to eat, engage, and invest in the week's agenda. She was sad (for a couple of days), but safe. We have incredible pictures and stories from that trip. We still talk about it both with fond and some sad remembrances. Fast-forward later into this same year. She's in the seventh grade. It's the annual seventh-grade class trip to Amsterdam, which is both educational and fun. She was a little less hesitant to leave this time, partly because she had a good friend now on the trip with her. But she was also a little less hesitant because she had one such independent venture under her belt. Still, her concerns over separating from her sisters and us were seemingly never ending. It's a wonder she didn't just wear us down to the point we literally threw in the towel with a resounding, "You win. Now just stay home and quit whining." But on the seventh-grade trip she did go!

One year later, now in the eighth grade, her class made their annual trip to the Ardennes Forest. Perhaps one of the most beautiful places in Europe, but not only that, the Ardennes is the scene of one of the most historical battles in WWII—a place where the Allies stopped the final Nazi thrust in the latter's attempt to turn the tide of the war back to Germany. It was a place where the Allies, led largely by American soldiers, fought hard for the freedom that we so enjoyed today, in horrible physical circumstances. Thousands of them died in the battle known as the Battle of the Bulge. Do you think this little piece of history had some impact on our pushing Shelby out the door on this trip? You bet it did. But guess who did not want to leave her sisters? Guess who did not want to leave her parents? Again! Even with two major trips in her repertoire. Guess who once again made the trip nonnegotiable? Yes. Those mean parents of hers.

I could spend a lot of ink here telling you all the wonderful outcomes of that trip and the two previously mentioned trips. But suffice to say one thing led to another. That is to say, one step led to another step that led to another step that led to another. When we moved to Houston and she knew NO one, Shelby managed. It was difficult. Perhaps ironically, her move to Houston was far more difficult than her move to Germany. No crystal ball was had when we moved to Germany. Who would have ever guessed that leaving *there* would be so difficult for Shelby? I am sure that she would have welcomed the departure heartily had we never pushed her out of the nest while living there. Moving back to the states brought its own enormous set of challenges, but I would say she was equipped in a way that she never would have been if we had acted conservatively and played into her emotions and wishes on all of those wonderful trips. Three years after coming to Houston, she left for college, a seven-hour drive away from her family. She went willingly and happily. And again, she has managed well.

♥ I am not suggesting it's always easy. I'm just suggesting that sometimes unwittingly, we create undesirable patterns of movement in our child's life. How? By never requiring them to leave us. Selfishly, we want them always close to us. To that end, maybe even unconsciously, we discourage them from participating in any activity that presents itself as one that would take them out of our clutches. We base this on what's comfortable for them *in the present*, and therefore, what's comfortable for us. If they don't want to learn to ride a bike, we say, "Ok, you don't have to." If they don't want to learn how to swim, we say, "Ok, you don't have to." If they don't want to attend summer camp of some sort, we say, "Ok, you don't have to." Do this often enough, and congratulations! You have effectively created a dependent, intimidated, overwrought child. You may indeed get what you want—that is for them to always remain close to you. But is it what's best for them? 🏚 And if you believe in God, is it what God wants for them? Is it possible for us as parents to so heavily influence the movements of our child as to actually interfere with God's plan for them? I believe that as long as I am able to make choices, I must believe, for my child's sake, the answer to that is yes! Let. Them. Go.

Insist on a summer activity that takes them away from you and requires them to engage with other adults and peers somewhat independently—to work out conflict, to experience new events and feelings, and situations. Let them expand their world.

In recent years, in the month of December, the girls and I decided to visit friends in Spain over the Christmas holiday. Shelby called and asked if I cared if she went ahead of her sisters and I, so that she would have a couple of extra days to visit her best friend who just happened to be in Germany at this same time. Since her break from college started sooner than her sisters' holiday breaks from high school, and since logistically and financially, it was okay with me. I said, "Sure, I can't see why not." We had prepared her for this moment, *whether or not in this moment* I was 100 percent comfortable. Certainly, the fact that Shelby lived overseas for four years lent itself to her level of comfort with this particular situation. True. *But don't miss the very important sequence of events here.* Up to this very moment in her life, we had been throwing Shelby into the deep end and telling her to swim. Her ability to fly to Europe ahead of us, negotiate all that goes with arriving at her destination, then flying to a different country to join up with us would never have happened—I am convinced—if we had not been willing to let her go to Beach Break when she was thirteen years old and absolutely dead set against it. Again—Let. Them. Go. And the sooner the better.

That's the sweet part of life though. To have the privilege of loving something or someone *so* much that you hurt when they're gone. Sadly, not everyone gets that opportunity. The enormous capacity that we have to feel loss and sadness owes only to our enormous capacity to love in the *first place.* How sweet is that? This should serve to lessen the blow of letting them go however difficult that may be.

💡 When they are toddlers, create some free spaces in the house where they can roam and play without borders, but under your watchful eye. Don't make them negotiate all of their toddler years in a twelve-by-twelve-foot space. Play outside in wide-open spaces as often as possible. As they get older, ease them into situations where they spend time away from you, but with other trusted adults. Then, when they are ready (as they will be now), send them to camp or other activity, again with trusted adults and organizers. You will be amazed (and frightened) at what they have the courage to do.

Spiraling or sauntering down a path with little life purpose is not the trajectory we want to set in motion for our children. What will it take for you, *the parent*, today to take hold of that compass and point them away from you? For me it just requires taking a look at the condition of the world we live in. Poverty, human trafficking, loss, and hardship that pervades our world and our communities—that tells me I need to raise world changers. Not just children who want what they can get for themselves, but what they can contribute. What would it take for you to let them go? What would it take for you to do everything in your power to catapult them into that direction? To facilitate their flight? It requires us as parents to set aside our own selfish wishes to have them close to us. And it also requires us to set aside even our maternal and paternal instincts of security and protection. Does that mean we throw caution to the wind? No! But we can no longer use those two tenets as excuses to keep our child from becoming everything that they are capable of becoming wholly separate and apart from us. Protection at the total expense of their self-initiative and self-sufficiency equals overprotection. Don't fall into this trap. Your willingness to navigate them through life stages in such a way that they quite naturally move forward and start navigating themselves into the world and out on their own will help transform them into healthy, confident, and capable adults. They will move more easily from that safe harbor of their home with us into a world where they can now make a home of their own.

VACATE THE PREMISES

W hat will it take for your son or daughter to vacate the premises? That is to say, move out? I know that there are legitimate situations where adult children remain at home. Sometimes the adult child or his parent, the breadwinner, loses their job. This in turn prompts the child to move in with his parents or vice versa. It is often the case, grown children need a place to live amidst transition. And in that case, they should have a clear plan with a clear timeline. But, for instance, if you're twenty-five, single, and gainfully employed, it's probably time to go. "Why?" you ask. "What if everyone is happy with the arrangement?" Indeed, what if parents and child do not mind? *That's exactly one of the reasons you need to go.* To fully become the person you are capable of being, to really know yourself, to truly be able to test and experience relationships in your life, to truly be able to grasp the responsibilities that go along with day-to-day household operation and taking complete care of yourself, it's paramount that you live on your own. It's even better if you can squeeze in a year or two of this prior to marriage. I think adjusting to sharing your life and emotions and your heart with a spouse, in such close quarters as marriage requires, it helps if we have been on our own first. Another reason to move out of your parents' house is this: there is a level of maturity that is simply unattainable when you don't. It's different meeting all of your own physical and emotional needs 24/7 than when your abode is with your parents. Sure, you're not a codependent, self-entitled kind of gal (hopefully not, because that makes this so much harder). But the fact is that inherently many of your needs are met by others when you live with them. If only your needs for socialization. When my niece first moved into her own apartment, one of the immediate emotions present was loneliness. But she got a dog, joined a church, met her neighbors, and cultivated her work relationships. Her apartment where she resided alone became just one element among all the elements of her life. It also became her home. Other needs met by your parents may (or may not) include meals, linens, clothing, utilities, insurance, vehicle, or electronics. It goes without saying they are meeting financial needs on some level even if you are paying them rent. I know it seems rather bossy and maybe even judgmental of me to suggest that if you are an adult still living at home with your parents, you need to move out. Again, this section is not trying to address *all* the legitimate reasons for that setup. What this section is trying to address are those adult children who have no real legitimate need for still living at home. Parents, start young pushing your kids out of the nest. This is truly a companion tip to the last one, "Fly Like an Eagle..."

💡 Because of course the younger you start teaching them independence and self-initiative, the more likely they will *want* to live away from home as an adult, which translates to *both* the parents and the child being able to negotiate and *navigate life on their own terms* in this next season of their lives.

CAN WE TALK?
TIP #23

PARENTING TIP #23:

HAVE IMPORTANT, AND POTENTIALLY LIFE-SAVING, AGE-APPROPRIATE CONVERSATIONS WITH YOUR KIDS

In every season of your child's life there are important conversations to have with them. Some of them concern taking care of themselves. Others concern taking good care of others. All of them are important. Some of them could literally save their life. Read on.

♥ When he's two years old, and you want him to learn to share, then have a discussion appropriate for a two-year-old about sharing in that moment you want him to do so. He's two. It's a simple conversation. "If you can't share your toys, you have to sit in time out." If you want your son to be respectful of women, then when he is a little guy, don't let him speak disrespectfully to his mom. Talk to him about the importance of his "mommy," and later when he is in high school or college, perhaps he will have a different opinion of women. If you want your girl to treat herself and her body with respect, then talk to her about how important she is to you (especially <u>you</u>, dad) and how important it is for her not to

71

compare herself or her body to others. If you want your daughter to avoid being a "mean girl," then discuss with her the importance of standing up for others and pay attention to moments when she gets her feelings hurt by others. Do not (I repeat, do NOT) see this as an opportunity to placate her or encourage her to be a victim. ("Oh, you poor little thing. I can't believe she said that to you. I'm calling her mother.") Rather, use it as a teaching opportunity. Now, more than any other time, when she has been offended by someone, your girl *knows* how another girl does *NOT* want to feel. Now more than ever, she knows how hurtful words and actions can be!

When *is* the last time you had a conversation with your son or daughter? A real one. Not a superficial conversation about after school pickup or football practice times, or "I'll be running late so eat dinner without me," or anything to do with the logistics of running a household, but a real conversation? "What happened in your day? What could you have done differently or what went well? What's the importance of treating others with respect? Summer vacation is soon here; how do you plan to balance leisure activity with serving in your community?" Conversations regarding the implications of those who choose to be sexually active early. Conversations about planning to be financially responsible and avoiding debt!

These are a just a few **life-saving** conversations. Obviously, not all of our hours can be devoted solely to these discussions. We are all busy. But you better believe that not allotting time in your busy schedules for these dialogues could be a powerful measuring stick for their future success and even their safety.

There has been such a plethora of reporting on sexual assault on college campuses in recent years, not to mention all of the sexual abuse and sexual harassment reporting and personal disclosure that has skyrocketed as a result of a recent social media campaign called "#MeToo!" A 2007 research study funded by the Department of Justice and prepared for the National Institute of Justice reported that *nearly* one in five undergraduate college women will be the victim of a sexual assault during college.[4] Other studies since that time have heralded that finding as a myth since the study only surveyed students from two (albeit very large) colleges. But as Alia Wong pointed out in her article, "Why the Prevalence of Campus Sexual Assault Is So Hard to Quantify," gathering data is a huge challenge due to politics, fear, and a lack of transparency in academic institutional policy.[5] The fact remains that our kids are and will be exposed to certain threats on a college campus and maybe even in their work environments, for which they may or may not be prepared. What does this mean to you as a parent of a girl or boy? Well, it might interest you to know that according to a DOJ study on campus sexual assault published December 2014,[6] the alleged college campus victims are primarily freshman females (think eighteen- or nineteen-year-old girls) and the alleged perpetrators are generally, repeat generally, male offenders who are students themselves at the college, three out of four of them known by the victim; not the stereotypical perpetrator: a stranger lurking in the bushes on campus. I refer to this to highlight the pervading need to talk with our kids. I wonder how many of those girls who were sexually assaulted had a literal discussion with their parent(s) about the hazards of attending drinking parties at college and a set of instructions on what to do and what not to do if you DO attend such a party. How many of these male coed perpetrators had a literal conversation with their parents about respecting women and about how to make wise choices when it comes to having sex or not having sex with someone who cannot give conscious, fully coherent consent?

What do we talk about in these "growing-up years" at home? We talk about everything under the sun. We talk about boys, girls, dating, school, expectations, coping with change, practicing manners, character, relationships, life and death, how to treat the opposite sex—everything! It's surreal to me to think or believe that simple (but substantial in content) conversations peppered throughout their childhood could save my child's life, keep her from being sexually assaulted, or maybe save her from bankruptcy.

Here's a few excerpts of such conversations, which can be *just a conversation*, or a conversation accompanied with action:

1. Never have revolving debt. Pay your bills in full each month. Other than a mortgage, the majority of debt drains your income and your financial resources, including your retirement savings. (Tip #43)

2. As a general rule, make good decisions when deciding whether or not to attend college parties which may or may not involve a bunch of strangers and a lot of alcohol. That is a lethal combination. And if you do attend such a party, you better never accept a drink from another person. Fix your own drink. Know that if you get drunk, while not necessarily illegal, still if you are incoherent, your odds of being sexually assaulted or even raped will greatly increase. Does that make the assault your fault? Absolutely not! *But it does mean you have it within your power to substantially lower your risk of being a victim.* Absolutely yes! Prevention is indicative of strength. Knowledge is power in this instance.

3. In your everyday interaction with others, remember that everyone, including you, is a human being, and deserves respect. "Seek first to understand, then to be understood."[7]

4. Don't walk alone through a deserted parking lot at night, and if you must, walk with purpose, head held high, looking around, no texting, have your keys out ready to get in the car, and go.

And the possibilities for "life-saving" conversations go on and on. So often, we parents lead lives that are very self-serving. Why do I think this? Because most of our time is spent centered around our children and their activities. That's the irony of the whole thing. We are with our kids a lot. But we are not really **with** them. We are not necessarily discussing with them what is important. Most of our commitments revolve around two things: our jobs (which pay the bills) and the daily orchestration (sometimes chaos) of getting our kids to their activities. There's little margin in such busy schedules for important family events such as eating dinner around the table, family game night, attending church together, or volunteering together. Unfortunately, however, statistics show that often-times these life-saving conversations happen in these *latter* places. We will discuss in Tip #47 how a strong correlation exists between the frequency of family dinners and a teenager's propensity to abuse drugs or alcohol. Furthermore, family meals eaten together at home are also connected to better report cards among teenagers and higher rates of high school grad-uation. Common Sense media, a nonprofit, nonpartisan organization, conducted a survey that found that *all* the parents surveyed (1,786 par-ents of children ages eight to eighteen living in the United States) spent nine-plus hours a day on all kinds of media, with eighty-two percent of that time dedicated to personal screen media alone, so eighty-two per-cent for leisure and personal, not work related. Ironically, seventy-eight percent of those parents felt they were *good* role models for their own children's media usage.[8] It bears noting that this ginormous amount of time devoted to all things media doesn't include going to work, cleaning the house, or ferrying your children to and from activities. Imagine after adding all of *that* time to your media time, what is left over? Bedtime? It is hard to believe there would be enough time left over to have these important life-saving conversations.

Not surprisingly, today's tweens and teens are matching their parents' screen time hour for hour and then some. These kiddos are spending almost as much time watching and surfing media devices as they might one day be expected to spend on a job! And lest you think it doesn't start until double digits, a survey conducted in March 2015 by the American Speech-Language-Hearing Association (ASHA) reported: "68% of the surveyed parents' 2-year-olds use tablets. Meanwhile, 59% use smart-phones, and 44% use video game consoles."[9] Seriously, there isn't a two-year-old on the face of this earth who needs to be using media in any form. An occasional movie for the two or three-year-old toddler of course is not going to ruin them. But we are starting them earlier and earlier with the acrid habit of media overload.

This then begs the lingering but grave question: Who's teaching them the dangerous implications of so much time spent on media? Who's having *that* conversation with them? And if both parents and children are spending this many hours glued to a screen, how could these sons and daughters possibly be spending quality time with parents and siblings and having meaningful conversations with them?

It's time for us as parents to make hard decisions about our family schedules, our children's activities, and our words. What are we going to say to them now *while the stakes are low*? Right now, they are housed inside the relative comfort and safety of our homes, but sooner than later, they will be out of our eyesight, out of our reach, and out of our comfort zone. What are we doing to prepare them for functioning in a world that indeed will not care nearly so much for their health and well-being as we do? How are we preparing them to be safe and successful on their own? No, of course, there are no foolproof ways of preparing your children for life on their own. No foolproof ways of ensuring their safety. But we can do better than mere minutes a week, which surely is all that's left once we are done with work, media time, and other, ostensibly necessary, activities that don't include our kids. Just as we have disposable income remaining after the bills are paid, so we have disposable time remaining after work is done. A good portion of that disposable time in our schedules would be well spent with our kids eating around the table, playing basketball with them, reading with them, or doing leisure activities together—than it is in front of the television or the computer.

Routing them from activity to activity is important and necessary. But this is an unlikely time and place for meaningful conversation to happen. *It could.* And yay if it does! But sometimes we just have to be **with** them and give one another undivided attention. *Prepare them for the inevitable events of life with your words.* Prepare them with practical conversations. Be intentional about family meals and family activities. As parents, we have the incredible privilege of having the most unique vantage point of our kids. A bird's eye view into their hearts. Insider information. For about the first twenty or so years, it's primarily our voice engaging them in thousands of conversations, shaping their character one way or the other. Dear God, let it be the voice of truth. Their success, but also their actual life, could depend on it.

ON VOLUNTEERING:
TIP #24

PARENTING TIP #24:

SERVE TOGETHER

F ind a place to serve with your children. Why do we even have to discuss this? It should be nonnegotiable. We have a practice in our house. Serving others. And participation is *nonnegotiable*. It's simple: serve someone beside yourself. It goes against the grain of our "self-serving, the busier the better, immediate gratification" kind of culture we live in. In an American society where kids are busier than they have ever been, and families don't have time for hospitality in their homes, much less service in their communities, it seems like a crazy—if not impossible—idea to incorporate volunteering into your family schedule. Call us nuts, I know. But we have this crazy idea that by serving others, our girls might grow up understanding that the world doesn't really revolve around them. We believe that serving others—and expressing altruism, generosity, and benevolence—will make our kids better people, better friends, better wives, better employees, colleagues, students... And, yes, we even believe it will make them happier. Yep! That's what we believe. At our previous church, once a month we participated in an "Adopt a Block" with our church. My kids have knocked on doors of houses of people they don't know to ask them if they need their yard mowed. Sometimes they just play in the park with the neighborhood kids. They have picked up trash along the roads, offered encouragement, and assisted those in need.

They have made other people feel important, cared for, and honored. My girls were never overzealous about getting up early on a Saturday morning to do this. And it was highly unlikely, at least at that point in their life, they would have decided to do this on their own without a little nudging from us! But remember? It's nonnegotiable! It's not an option.

Along with this same ministry, our old church "adopted" a nursing home. It was a challenge to know what to say and do initially! Awkward is the word that comes to my mind. But to serve is to be stretched way outside of our comfort zones. That's the sweet spot for your kids. That's when suddenly, they realize that in this very moment, "my needs have been trumped, overruled." By who? Well, maybe a little ten-year-old in the park who wants to play tag, or an elderly person confined to a wheelchair, or the homeless guy at the busy intersection near our house. And the best part is, our girls always step up. They do it. They survive the discomfort. They handle it. And they are happier for it. They learn huge lessons about those in need. They learn even bigger lessons about themselves, and what they are capable of doing.

💡 Start small if necessary. Make your kids hand wash the dinner dishes, vacuum, sort laundry; teach them—**no, require them**—to be servants in their *own* home. First make *that* nonnegotiable. Then it won't be so foreign of an idea to serve **outside** their home. If your kids are like mine, they spend plenty of time serving themselves. Facilitate opportunities for them to serve others. Simple ways like taking cookies to your next-door neighbors is an easy way to start. And when you do, make it nonnegotiable! We live in a very broken world. One astonishingly full of much violence, hate, and discord. Get angry about it. Fight back. Help a shut-in with her yard. Make cookies to welcome a new neighbor. Offer to keep someone's kids for them when they are packing out to move. Handwrite a note of encouragement to a friend. Handwrite a birthday card for a dear friend. Just do it!

We started this practice of serving others outside of our home and inside our home years ago. Now the girls are serving on their own. They find ways to be involved in their communities at college and in their respective churches. It was because we stuck to this principle all the years of their childhood, that they *now* have a natural desire to give back to others around them. They now take the initiative to serve. For them, it's a joy and not just about a tax deduction or making my mom happy. It makes their heart happy.

"God has given each of you a gift from his great variety of spiritual gifts. Use them well to serve one another"

(1 PETER 4:10, NLT)

THE SEX TALK:
TIP #25

MAKE THE SEX TALK A TWO-WAY CONVERSATION

Make the sex talk a two-way conversation with your child. Right now it is a ONE-WAY discussion between the culture your child lives in and your child. We need to give the choice back to our kids. They need to be reminded that they are allowed to say no. Open up the dialogue. It doesn't matter what your own past choices were or were not. Don't lord your past over your kids. **And refer back to Tips #1 and #8.** We live in a world that is having a one-way conversation with our kids. That one-way conversation is this: "You will have sex before marriage. That's 'normal,' a given; the only question that remains then is, how soon it will happen?" Read the headlines of popular magazines while waiting to check out at the grocery store. Watch a pop rock music video. Follow your kid's favorite celebrity on twitter. Read an article in *Seventeen* magazine. Read an article in *Cosmopolitan* magazine. Watch a movie. I challenge you to find **one** piece of media—TV show, magazine article, movie, any TV ad spot, anywhere, anytime—that simply says, "Um… You have a choice. You *can* say no to sex…" Show me one. Okay, maybe the abstinence message built into my girls' sixth-grade health class curriculum. Or maybe the various "Let's Wait" programs found for teens in faith-based religions. But from a media source? No! We have taken a little bit of an unorthodox approach with our kids with regard to this subject matter. We actually told them, "Yes, you *can* have sex before marriage." Undoubtedly that is true. But (and here's the clincher) you don't *have* to! And then we have followed that up with a healthy dose of unconditional love, boundaries, natural consequences for their behaviors, right and wrong, and a great, big open door to come tell us ANYTHING. We fully understand that this ugly, self-centered, self-gratifying world that we live in—the one who craves immediate gratification in all of life and sells that tenet in advertising—is sending ONE message to our girls. "You *will* have sex before marriage. The only question is when." Like I said, it's a one-way conversation. We realized quickly that we needed to make it a two-way conversation. We did a simple thing, guided by our faith and convictions, and as importantly, a deep-seated love for our precious daughters; we did the only sensible thing we could do. *We gave them back the choice.* We told them, "Oh, and by the way, you can say no!" This is something that everyone can sink their teeth into, regardless of your faith, your belief systems, or your political position. Giving our kids a choice is certainly something we can all agree on. So why then do most parents conform to this cultural message about their kids, effectively taking that choice away? Because sex in our culture is an easy sell. The message is embedded in a self-gratifying culture that we live and function in every day, and therefore is part and parcel of the very fabric of our lives. Sometimes it's easier to go along with the "Joneses" than it is to have such serious conversations with our kids beyond the ones that just cover the day's logistics. For instance, "I'll pick you up from school at 3:00. Don't forget you have a dentist appointment at 3:30." *But* if we all know and agree that having sex too early, too young, and outside of a loving, intimate relationship is emotionally damaging to our kids, then why aren't more of us making this a two-way discussion? Why are we sticking our heads in the sand and allowing *total strangers* to have so much power and influence over our children's decision about their sexuality, their worth, and their potential to succeed in life? It may be because no one ever talked to *us* about this important subject matter. As children, many of us were thrown to the wolves when it came to learning about sex and sexuality. But that doesn't mean we should perpetuate that cycle. It could be because we are too dang busy. Who has time for "special weekends," family dinners at the kitchen table, board games, family vacations? It could be that we have allowed our children to watch rated-R movies and TV since, well, I don't know when, or that your kid has had a total access pass to someone's pornographic magazine collection, and the mind-set has already been set in stone. Maybe it's a combination of all the above, and consequently, you don't feel adequate in having this loving and honoring conversation with your son or daughter.

Don't believe that lie! No one loves your child like you do, with the one exception of their Creator. And God is greater than all of our mistakes. So wade into the waters with your babies. Be a spiritual leader in their life. Be their champion. For God's sake, don't give that job away.

Okay, say we don't buy into the lie that almost everyone will have sex prior to marriage. *What does that mean and what does it not mean?*

1. It *doesn't* mean you lie to your kids about your own sexual virtue (Tip #7). If you were not a virgin before you were married, for goodness sakes, tell them the truth when the inevitable can no longer be avoided. You can bet the question is going to come up. Lying to our kids is treacherous ground and makes navigating through life situations in the ensuing years very difficult. There were a lot of things I did as a teenager and a young person that I don't want my children to do. I mean—think about it. If you were a recovered narcotics addict, would you say, "Well, I did it, so my kids will, too!" On the contrary, you would be all the wiser about those choices and their consequences. And you can and should share that information with your kids at age-appropriate times and in the right setting.

2. It also *doesn't* mean you abdicate the responsibility of sex education for your children. C'mon, parents! Put your big girl and big boy pants on and talk to them. They want to hear it from

you. They might not act like it. But if you want your girl to learn about sex and *ALL* that is involved in her sexuality from "Johnny boy," the kid in her ninth-grade biology class, then don't tell her anything. "Johnny boy" will most certainly take care of that for you. Just know that if you don't, sadly someone else will! And the likelihood of that being emotionally devastating for your son or daughter is great. *On the other hand, this doesn't mean you have to reject the school's established curriculum covering this subject.* It just means that if you have already covered it with your child, there won't be any surprises. All of our daughters were present in their respective health classes for the subject matter, and they were no worse for the wear for being there and participating in that curriculum. In fact, the curriculum they sat through was pretty benign. Our input was much more formidable and descriptive. As it should be.

3. It *does* mean that if you are the mom, you designate a "special weekend" with your girl, just you and her. If you can, go out of town. If you can't, do a day trip or have everyone else in the family leave the house for the weekend. Give yourselves time to prepare. Have her write down questions or listen to helpful commentaries that you like from trusted teachers/counselors about sex and sexuality beforehand. Get some help with where to start. *Passport to Purity* is a great source,[10] but there are many! Go out to eat. Shop. Do something fun. Send her the message that she is precious and special to you, that she is special to her Creator. I think sixth or seventh grade is a great time to do this with your girl or boy. It should closely coincide with the onset of puberty. I wouldn't do it much earlier or later than this. *Likewise*, it means if you are the dad, you do the special weekend trip with your son. Prepare in the same way moms do with their girls. Tell him how special he is to you and his Creator. You answer his questions and talk to him about your expectations, and you also teach him how to treat women, starting with his mom and

sisters, and then of course other girls and women. Buy a special small gift or piece of jewelry for your son or daughter at the end of the weekend, which reminds them how much they are loved and cared for, and that their purity is honorable and healthy.

"Everything is permissible for me, but not everything is beneficial. Everything is permissible for me, but I will not be mastered by anything"

(1 CORINTHIANS 6:12, CSB)

"Or do you not know that your body is the temple of the Holy Spirit who is in you, whom you have from God, and you are not your own? For you were bought at a price; therefore, glorify God in your body and in your spirit, which are God's"

(1 CORINTHIANS 6:19–20, NKJV)

"I have the right to do anything," you say—but not everything is beneficial. "I have the right to do anything"—but not everything is constructive"

(1 CORINTHIANS 10:23, NIV)

I see kids all the time who are disconnected from the people who love them the most. When my kids were in junior high, I saw unbelievable sexual text messages to my own girls from other teens (boys and girls), and unbelievable sexual posts on social networks by tweens and teens. But I rarely ever see these latter kids lose their social networking privileges. Be involved with your teen. They need to know there is no person on earth who loves and cares for them like you. For them to know that, we have to actually spend time with them. Passing them like ships in the night doesn't give them what they need from us. Having conversations is a good start. (Tip #23) And when it comes to their sexuality, love them enough to make this a two-way discussion. Reverse this cultural message they get clobbered with every single day. Give them back the choice.

Dads and Dating:
Tips #26–27

GIRLS NEED THEIR DADS, PERIOD

At some point, I remember vividly, I was dislodged, ousted, extricated by my girls as the center of their universe, and replaced by Dad. It was natural and normal. I couldn't stop it or influence it. Which begs the question, what happens to girls when they hit that developmental milestone, and Dad is absent (emotionally and physically)? Girls require the unconditional acceptance and appropriate touch that dads render. I believe this may possibly be the most significant informer of their choices in relationships, sex, and marriage (Tip #25). Maybe you're a single parent. Hopefully, Dad is still present and engaged. If not, find a role model. A stand-in. A loving and trusting male, maybe another dad who has time to mentor another "daughter." In any case, refer back to Tip #1. This is paramount for our girls. This is a short and sweet tip, but it packs a huge punch. If girls have a male father figure in their life who loves them unconditionally and gives them appropriate touch and attention, the likelihood that they will try to fill that huge, gaping hole with the sexual attention of an underserving boy (or girl) is so much less. I love my husband for a million reasons, but perhaps the character trait in him that I appreciate more than anything is the devotion and attention that he has paid to our three daughters since their births. He has given them as much or more than I have ever contributed to them emotionally. He has given them the love of a father, and he has modeled for them the relentless and unending love of their heavenly Father.

DON'T ENCOURAGE
(OR EMBRACE) DATING

I never said you'd agree with all my parenting tips. This doesn't mean your teens won't "go out" with someone all on their own initiative. It doesn't mean they won't date. But you don't have to be cheering it on, either. This is an especially destructive practice when they are tweens and younger. But really, teenagers don't need to date, either. Kids and teens need to understand their intrinsic worth and that their confidence isn't contingent upon whether or not they have a boyfriend or girlfriend (God help us). And parents need to understand the same thing. Spend time emphasizing the importance of relationships with family and friends. And model *that* true love for them along the way.

> "It is possible for everyone to find the deepest unity of
> heart and soul without marriage."
> —Heini Arnold

Amen! We need to quit sending the message to our kids that their value lies ultimately in their ability to either lasso a boyfriend, girlfriend, husband, or wife! Some of my single Christian friends needed to hear this, and sadly the American church has too often been unwilling to say it.

But nevertheless, back to dating. When we take time to ponder this, does it really make sense to put a sixteen-year-old boy alone in a room with a sixteen-year-old girl? And then expect him (or her) to behave himself? It's sort of like putting an alcoholic in a room alone with multiple bottles of liquor and telling him, "Don't taste." I know that seems extreme and dramatic. But what's wrong with boys and girls hanging out in groups when they are young? And when they do choose to "date," if they are still minors and living at home, make sure they know the boundaries and the rules you have in place. This certainly has to do with age, but it also has to do with maturity. Just approach dating with caution and care. Never ever send the message to your child that they should and could have a boyfriend or girlfriend because they are so good looking or because they deserve it. What they deserve more than anything at this age is the time and attention of their parents.

DEATH AND LIFE:
TIP #28

TAKE THEM TO FUNERALS

As I mentioned earlier, when I was only five years old, my parents drowned in a fishing accident. This was my earliest memory of a funeral that I attended. And it was my parents' funeral. I still remember that vividly, but honestly, it's not a bad memory. Their death is a negative memory, no doubt. But their funeral is not. My mother's mother had endured death and loss in her family life so many times already, that when my parents died, I don't think it ever crossed her mind to prevent my sisters and me from being at that funeral. For her, death was as natural as life, and she obviously believed that funerals were the capitulation of life, a necessary ritual serving as a way of saying good-bye and honoring the loved one. I don't think there is anything wrong with taking a child to a funeral who is old enough to know and recognize for years to come that this person was in my life and now she is not. One of our nieces was never taken to funerals as a child or a teenager. There were opportunities to do so. Elderly family members passed away. Great-aunts and uncles. Sometimes church members succumbed to old age. But she and her sisters were always left at home with a caregiver, or when old enough to stay home alone, they just stayed behind. I think that was a lost opportunity. Sadly, the first funeral my niece attended was her own daughter's. She lost a child to a genetic disorder at five weeks old. When she told me that she had never been to a funeral, I was stunned. It was enough to be grieving the loss of a child, but for funerals to be such uncharted territory made the task of burying their baby so much more daunting. Recently, a very close friend of mine lost her brother in a car accident. Her son, five years old, wanted to go to the funeral. She relented and let him attend his uncle's funeral. It was a positive experience amidst a tragic time. If we never ever allow our children to attend funerals, we may be sending them the message that death is to be feared. The fact is, death is inevitable. The less we fear it, the better. When our children were younger and someone in our church would die, we would take them to the funeral. When their grandfather died, we took them to the funeral. It wasn't their first one. We talked to them openly about the funeral itself and their feelings and emotions that surfaced. We let them ask questions and answered them as best we could.

"Precious in the sight of the Lord is the deaths of His faithful servants"

(PSALM 116:15, NIV)

It's hard for us to imagine there is anything precious about death, especially in the event that people suffered before they died. Certainly, there is nothing precious about that. But this Psalm seems to indicate that the passing from death to life is for God, like crossing over a bridge into something much better and more beautiful than anything we could ever hope or imagine. Whether you believe in God or not, and whether you believe in an afterlife with your Creator or not, still this Psalm depicts a different picture of death than the one that we so often fear.

Letting your children attend funerals may not be the most pleasant part of parenting. But when you do it together, and you are present with them in that moment, you are truly giving them the tools to deal with the death of loved ones, or perhaps even deaths still to come, yours or their own, in the most sensible and loving way you know how.

Parenting Quarrels:
Tip #29

LET THEM SEE YOU ARGUE DON'T LET THEM SEE YOU WAGE WAR

M arriage is tough. I think most would agree when I say, "Once we had children, it got a lot tougher." Why is that? Well, we know why. When they are young, you're sleep deprived. As they get older, the challenge of staying on the same page with each other when it comes to discipline, activities, working, and sharing responsibilities becomes a challenge. Not only do we bring different ideas to the marriage of how holidays should be spent but we also bring different ideas to the marriage of how to parent. But by far the biggest reason why marriage becomes tougher after having children is simply because of the demands on our time. Before we only had our jobs and perhaps hobbies to compete for our time together. Now that you have children, it seems like chaos rules and intimacy suffers. Children stir up a LOT of emotions, as well. Furthermore, if your marriage was in a rocky place *before* having children, that is typically aggravated when children are introduced into the mix. Okay, where's the bright side in this tip? The point is, as parents, we are going to fuss and quarrel. It's the nature of the beast. It's okay for our kids to see us argue, especially if we are good at establishing boundaries and if we have good conflict-resolution skills. But I don't think they should be a witness to drop-down, heavy-duty screaming matches and certainly they should not be a witness to verbal or physical abuse between their parents. We have been guilty a few times of having a screaming match in front of our girls. I have always regretted that. News flash! Our kids know that we are not perfect. They expect us to have disagreements with one another. But they are hopeful that we know how to act as mature adults and work through those disagreements. If you are married or divorced, this is absolutely true for both of you. Divorce is inherently tough enough on kids, but if the two of you cannot get along, and if you are always unreasonable with one another in front of the kids, or, God forbid, you pit your child against your spouse or ex-spouse with degrading words and fabrications, your child will suffer. Perhaps you only intend for your spouse or ex-spouse to suffer. But that is delusional. Your child will suffer, as well. And mightily. Therefore, if you feel like your arguing is out of control, and neither of you knows how to rein it in, then seek counseling. If you're reading this, and you feel like you have good conflict-resolution skills with the other parent of your child, then make sure that you are intentional about maintaining those skills. And be sure to let your kids know that though you don't agree on everything, you will indeed be taking a united front with their father (or mother) when it comes to their (your son's or daughter's) best interest. It's important to remember we are going to argue with each other, but it's necessary that when it comes to our children learning how to behave in relationships, how they see us argue—with grace, forgiveness, and resolution seeking, all of these things—will absolutely shape their own relationship behaviors.

Don't let problems in your marriage go unchecked. I have had problems in my marriage. Indeed, sometimes I have been the problem. I have close friends and mentors with whom I can talk and in whom I can confide. I don't seek out the counsel of friends and mentors to lambast my husband, but rather to seek counsel and advice. I need trustworthy people to show me and tell me how to be a better marriage partner, the same as I need trustworthy people to tell me how to be a better parent (Tip #1). This goes for men, too. Women are much more likely to seek out counsel and encouragement from other women. Men often see this as a weakness, and well, they are just less likely to ask another male to hold them accountable in their marriage. That isn't fair to their spouse or their marriage. It isn't even fair to themselves. This parenting tip is about "letting your kids see you argue, but not letting them see you wage war" with each other. Moreover, it begs the examination, "does my marriage need a checkup?" An "every so often" marriage checkup aids the former. Our kids are going to learn from us. If we are verbally abusive to one another, they are likely going to repeat this behavior at home and away from home in other relationships, as well. If we learn to fight fair in our marriages, and if we learn to express our feelings constructively with each other, say we are sorry when necessary, and grant forgiveness as we should, we are equipping our own kids with the tools they need to do the same.

WISHY-WASHY PARENTING: TIP #30

KNOW THE DIFFERENCE BETWEEN MAKING A SUGGESTION AND GIVING MARCHING ORDERS

Showing your child two different paint colors to choose from is a suggestion. Telling him to unload the dishwasher is a marching order. One day I was doing some shopping at a wholesale store when I heard a wild commotion. A toddler was standing up in the cart while his mom was *suggesting* he sit down. If you're at all familiar with the floors in a wholesale store, you know that they are hard concrete. Sure enough, after a very long two- or three-minute ordeal of the child standing up in the cart screaming and the mom *suggesting* he sit down, the child fell headlong onto that concrete floor. It was terrifying. Poor mom was mortified. Several people in the store rushed over to her side. He was crying to beat the band, but he appeared okay. It was certainly enough of an injury that it merited monitoring for the next twenty-four hours in case he had a concussion. Before it happened, I wanted to just run over and give the mom a quick tip about the difference between a suggestion and a marching order, *and not only the difference* but when to use one versus the other. In this case, the child was just a toddler. Geez, just pick him up physically and set him down in the cart. Toddlers don't really get suggestions. Their brains don't really process that efficiently. We are to be hands-on parents with toddlers, and I am not talking about spanking. Just pick him up and set the boy in the cart. If it is impossible on that day to get through the store with his cooperation intact, then you might have to leave the store that day and go home. It happens. It's okay.

But I wouldn't do either of the following two things: 1) I wouldn't let him put himself in danger by standing up or moving around in that cart unsecured, and 2) I wouldn't reward him for his screaming behavior. Say no to bribes as a reward for throwing a fit. If not, your child will learn the one pattern of behavior that gets him what he wants every single time. That's why sometimes just leaving the place is the best option. If she doesn't stop screaming or you cannot gain her cooperation, better to have your shopping plans thwarted until another day than it is to reward said behavior. And better to go home without a knot on their head if you can help it.

If you have a sink full of dishes and you want your child to do the dishes, then don't make a suggestion. Use language that is respectful but forthright. Teenagers recognize and exploit wishy-washy behavior. They will take your wishy-washy self out at the knees with both their words and their total lack of compliance. We may say things like, "Katie, I want you to hand wash. Halle, I want you to clear. Shelby, finish wiping down the countertops. And we need it done now." We make it clear this is not a suggestion. It's a marching order. Why is this important? Well, in the case of the toddler in the wholesale store, this parenting technique directly impacted his safety. In the case of teenagers and all children, they need to be respectful of their parents and themselves. When we constantly do everything for them (Tips #4 and #10), it tends to facilitate a lot of narcissism and a lack of compassion for others. And finally, sometimes, something just needs to be done. Our kids need (not just want) certain things from us. They need us to provide housing and food for them. And when they are young, they need us to schedule doctor appointments for them, to make sure they are registered for school, and a thousand other things. But indeed, *we actually need* (not just want) *things from them, as well.* We need them to do dishes. We need them to put their laundry away. We need them to complete homework, feed the dog, put gas in the car, and a host of other things that require marching orders—not just suggestions.

💡 If we insist on suggesting to our toddlers and little children tasks that we *need* them to do, not *just want* them to do, then we are going to have teenagers whose existence revolves around their own desires. They will truly continue to take everything from you. But it will be more and more difficult to get them to give back. It will be more and more difficult for you to garner their participation in family life and activities. And it will be more and more difficult to convince them to complete the tasks that make your family not only run more smoothly and efficiently but also tasks that when done provide the opportunity for having fun together. If you are a parent who cannot give marching orders, and so you constantly make suggestions in places where you should be giving commands, change your habits. Be intentional about it. If you are a parent of a teenager and you've already been giving only suggestions for a long time, it is not too late. You can even have a family meeting and say:

> *"Some things are going to change. We have noticed that when we ask you to _____ (do the dishes, unload the dishwasher, mow the yard, turn in your homework), you don't do it. Perhaps this is partly our fault by not being firm enough about this in the first place. But we feel like that lackadaisical attitude on both our parts has not served either our family's best interest or your best interest. So now we are going to require you to be more intentional about doing what we ask you to do when we ask you to do it—without excuses or complaints. And if you are not compliant, there will be a loss of privileges."*
> *(Then name or list those privileges. Make it real for them.)*

This is a suggested dialogue to have with your teenager who is only accustomed to getting suggestions. Or this is a proposed dialogue to have with *any* teenager who struggles with marching orders.

💡 Furthermore, if you are parents of little ones, be the parent *now* who knows the difference between giving suggestions and giving marching orders. Recognize that they are the child and you are the parent. This requires you as a parent to draw a few lines in the sand.

We often get looks of shock and wonder when our kids do things we need them to do without asking. For instance, when we have dinner company and the girls just start clearing the table on their own, without being asked. It's not unusual for our guests to ask us, "How did you get them to do that?" Recently, we were at a party with friends, and at the end of the meal my girls started helping clear the table along with their friend who was the daughter of our host. Our gracious host got onto them a little bit, saying, "Quit, you're guests!" But it was truly just a habit for them. And they didn't mind. It did not occur to them that they may have broken etiquette. Our kids know the difference between suggesting a restaurant for dinner and telling them they must pack their suitcase for a trip *now*. They know the difference between choosing a paint color for their room and unloading the dishwasher. They also know the difference in my tone of voice when I ask them, "What do you want for Christmas?" versus when I say, "I need you to take out the trash." One is a suggestion. The other is a marching order.

CHILL:
TIP #31

PARENTING TIP #31:

BE PLAYFUL

Serious is necessary a lot of the time. Conversations about their studies, their curfews, their friends, sex, drinking, and other conversations with our children require a serious dialogue (see Tip #23). But if we are unable to be playful, our kids will only know the staunch rule following you, not the lighthearted, playful, humorous you. You might say, "I don't have a lighthearted, playful, humorous side." But inside all of us there is a humorous person just laughing to get out. How do I know this? Because I am a parent who errs on the side of serious. Cautious; left brain more than right. When my children were born and as they grew into toddlers and then little girls, I found it not adequate for me to simply be sitting on the couch while they went about their playtime on the floor or in their rooms. It wasn't always enough for me to be in the kitchen as they carried on in their imaginary games in the next room. NO, I found myself on the floor with them—eye level—tickling or laughing or playing imagination with them. We read countless books together and mimicked the characters, laughing at each other and ourselves. No, I couldn't always be involved in their playtime. I had cooking and chores and work. *Nor* would I have wanted to always invade that space. It was certainly necessary for them to learn how to occupy themselves without constant adult involvement. And they were very good at playing alone and with each other. I loved that! But sometimes it was absolutely necessary for me or their dad to get down on their level and just be playful.

💡 Having done this a lot with my girls as toddlers, it was an easier jump to being playful with them as teenagers, but more challenging. Because teenagers by nature become less playful, more difficult, busier, and sassier. And our girls have been no exception to this. So not only did Paul and I both have jobs and many other obligations, the girls had extracurricular activities, jobs, and school, as well. And teenagers as we all know can be difficult to decipher emotionally! But being playful was still just as important as ever. I have mentioned board games several times in this book. It applies here, as well. Playing Monopoly or Yahtzee or card games is playful. Silly dancing in the living room (in a way that would not be good in public) also happens occasionally in our house. Paul is really good about engaging the girls with humor. In fact, he is so good, he thinks he is terribly hilarious when he isn't. Which is really, really funny. Our kids need to be able to take care of things and be on task. They need our seriousness for discipline and for working out conflicts. But they need our humor, too. It's vital to our relationship to often express our love for them though humor.

Humor also works great as a distraction strategy and occasionally an appropriate alternative to discipline, especially for younger children. Once when Shelby was about ten years old, we were visiting our good friends whose daughter had an appointment, which had been previously scheduled, to go horseback riding. Shelby was very sad and naturally complaining a little about wanting to go along, which clearly, she could not. At first, I started to feel that familiar pang of anxiety rising up and sensed awkwardness for our friends who felt bad she could not go. I entertained the idea that discipline for a bad attitude was forthcoming. Then suddenly I had another thought and, with a lot of drama, threw myself down on the floor and said, "Shelby, do you want to ride a horse? Well, hop on, girl!" And hop on she did, gleefully. Sure, this was hard on Mom's back and thankfully Dad took over. Humor, in lieu of an alternate disciplinarian tactic or scolding, worked its magic in that situation. She felt loved and cared for when I threw myself down on that floor on all fours (yeah, like an idiot) and made awful horse impressions. But honestly, her little friend went to her horse-riding appointment and we never heard another lament from Shelby over that.

Just a few days ago, my husband said to me, "When I think about girls whose father never played tickle monster with them, it breaks my heart." Humor. Funny. Playful. Ridiculous. Hope. Love. Understanding. Acceptance. Our kids need us to be playful. If this comes naturally for you, great. In fact, if you are really prone to be playful, you may have to be on guard lest you find you cannot be the disciplinarian you need to be. But if you are a parent, like me, who is prone to seriousness and really struggle to be playful, change that! You can do it. Be intentional about being playful both in word and in deed. Your children will love it. Perhaps they'll see a side of you they've not known before. But it is sure not to disappoint.

YES, YOU CAN!
TIP #32

SAY YES AS OFTEN
AS POSSIBLE

S ay yes as often as possible. Saying no is very important, but saying yes is just as important. Not that you will be saying yes to outrageous requests like, "Can I have a new car?" Or, "Can I stay out with my boyfriend all night?" No! Say yes when they are little and ask if they can go outside to play. It's always better than watching an image on a screen. Say yes as often as you can when they are asking you to join them in an activity. "Mom, do you want to play a game?" "Mom, do you want to go get coffee?" "Dad, do you want to go for a walk?" Say yes when they hang out in your bedroom longer than you'd like at bedtime because you are really, really tired and just want to retreat into a quiet slumber. But instead shrill voices are yelling in your ear and rolling around all over your space. Say yes! Say yes when you know in your heart a yes is appropriate and as far as you are able to afford it, it doesn't break the bank or infringe on other necessary and essential activities. As my girls have grown up, I have said yes to amusement parks, and county and state fairs. At some point, having ridden my millionth roller coaster and driven my zillionth bumper car, I know I had seen the last amusement park that I ever hoped to see. But it did not break the bank, and I had the privilege of saying yes! It was not convenient for my liking, in that it was not something *I* would have chosen for a fun activity. But they asked me, and I couldn't think of one single, solitary good excuse for saying no! Except for the possible fact that it was inconvenient.

Why is it important to say yes as often as possible? One reason is obvious. If the question involves you as a parent spending time with your child, then we should *always* say yes *as often* as possible. What a great comfort and beautiful message to send them. "I love spending time with you. It's so much fun." And what a gift to us when our son or daughter *wants to spend time with us.* Exploit this every chance you get. And the other reason for saying, "Yes, you can," or, "Yes, we can," is born out of that word *can.* When they ask a question such as, "Can I play with Joey this afternoon?" or "Can I color?" or "Mom, can I help you in the kitchen?" they are in effect asking, **"Am I capable of playing and interacting with others in a positive way? Can I problem solve? Can I cook? Can I fix stuff?"** So then, when we do say yes as often as possible, we are *unwittingly* sending them another important message: "You are capable of so much." *As we give them our affirmative answer, we are also giving them affirmation.* Wow! All of that can happen with just the answer yes? Yes, it can!

We said yes as often as possible to our girls when they were growing up, and in recent years they have shot back with uncanny abilities such as traveling alone, eliminating drama in their social circles, leading Bible studies, separating easily from us and working, leading, and volunteering on their own.

💡 Who knew that all of those times we were simply saying yes to playdates, yes to messing up the house, yes to cleaning up the house, yes to making a mess in the kitchen, yes to going outside in the rain, yes to the county fair, yes to Six Flags amusement park, we were actually teaching them how to say yes to opportunities, mission trips, and volunteerism? Who knew that we were teaching them to say, "I can do this. I am capable. I am smart, and I am a problem solver." Say no when you must. That is absolutely important, but by all means say **yes** as often as possible. And watch them blossom into incredibly capable, confident, and creative individuals.

MANAGE THEIR MEDIA:
TIPS #33–35

FOR PETE'S SAKE, MONITOR THEIR SOCIAL NETWORKING

W hat's wrong with the idea of sticking to the general rule of requiring your child to be thirteen years old before they are allowed to have social networking accounts? Really, parents, what's the worst thing that is going to happen? They might actually have to wait for something in a culture that teaches us to "hurry and grow up," and "immediate gratification gives you everything you want."

So, Rule 1: Make them wait until they are thirteen years old (or older). They will survive. I promise.

Rule 2: Set up guidelines. The interesting thing about setting up guidelines for our children and their social networking is that as adults we are responsible for following the same guidelines. If we are going to tell our child they are not allowed to drop the "F" bomb on Instagram or Facebook, then we can't, either. And, YES, that includes this "F_____." That might be the most ridiculous misconception on the part of adults (young and old). That is to say, "If I only put the first letter, then I am not *really* saying or typing the word." Good grief. Look, I know everyone, and their brother uses expletives and profanity as part and parcel of their everyday life. Sometimes I think adults see this as total access to teenagers.

"If I use this language, then I am showing them that I can step into their world. They will trust me." That's hogwash. Call me old fashioned. But I think it lacks class. It is vulgar, unprofessional, and just because it is "normal" doesn't make it okay. By and large, employers still want to hire men and women who know how to engage others in conversation in a professional and articulate manner, having a strong vocabulary that is not riddled with expletives. That includes in person and on their social networking sites.

As I wrote this section, I researched and read so many articles and studies on the subject of social networking sites. It was overwhelming. I wanted to talk about and reference all of those findings, but in the end, I realized that just what *I know* about the social media accounts of my daughter's peers is sometimes appalling and disturbing. For instance, girls in her high school who regularly use their phones for "sexting." Sexting (or "sex texting") is the sending or receiving of sexually explicit or sexually suggestive images, messages, or video via a cellphone or the Internet. Moreover, the numbers of teenagers in our top-ranked high school who are using their devices for bullying, slander, "hooking up," breaking up, and a host of other things that DON'T include anything educational or productive is ridiculous. I bet most of you can report the same news about your child's junior high or high school. Private or public.

So back to Rule 2: Set up guidelines. Guidelines also extend to the classroom. Teenagers in high schools across this country are literally addicted to their phones. Steve Gardiner is a high school English teacher and a national board-certified teacher in Billings, Montana. In an article that he wrote for *Education Week*, he noted:

> "In a career that spans 38 years, I have not seen any single diversion that so distracts students from reading, writing, thinking, and working. When the cellphone is in front of them, they are completely focused on it. When the cellphone is in the backpack, they are worried because they can't see it. On the first day of class, I tell them that if they can't go 57 minutes without checking their cellphones, they have a problem

and need to seek professional help. They laugh. I laugh, but I know how true that is. Only when I tell them to take their cellphones and put them inside their backpacks do they start to understand how accurate my diagnosis is."[11]

It is truly scary. Parents, tell your kids they canNOT have their phones out during instruction without the permission of their teacher. They canNOT social network in class. They canNOT have their earbuds in their ears while the teacher is instructing. If you think your child has never done this, ask them. (Not reproachfully, just curiously and with true interest.) You might be very surprised at what you discover. Teens can be very rude in their classrooms by refusing to part from their phone during classroom instruction or while doing classwork. This is unacceptable behavior.

Rule 3: You cannot air out all of your problems and anger on social networking. This discourages our children from exerting any effort at effective problem solving. They opt instead to hide behind the screen. People who air out their anger against the world and others on social networking, generally speaking, are incapable of confronting someone in person in an effective, grown-up way, and are incapable of seeking long-term conflict resolution. **IF** we are capable as adults of monitoring our OWN social networking, being mature about what we post and not using profanity, *then we can and should absolutely expect these same social networking behaviors from our children.* **IF** as a parent we have the courage to monitor our child's Instagram, Facebook, Twitter, or other account, then it is highly probable that we might *also* help them avoid a lot of possible heartaches. The fallout of your bad social networking behaviors could be lost relationships, lost jobs, lost job interviews, college rejection, scholarship rejection, hurt and disappointment with people you care about, and just the risk of making yourself look like an idiot. Is the latter what we want for our children? No, I don't think so. I think we want to raise children who are capable of engaging their peers and adults in a classy, sensible way, using both their constructive words and decency, both in person *AND* electronically. I would suggest that before you disable your child's ability to have healthy and functional relationships, disable their electronic devices.

Social networking serves a great purpose. I love the ability we have to stay in touch with our loved ones virtually all over the world. What I don't love is how social networking has replaced necessary personal contact with others, and in many cases replaced decency in our lives with indecency. Get on board with this tip, parents. Among parenting tips, this one is crucial.

FOR PETE'S SAKE,
LIMIT THEIR SCREEN TIME 💡

Lately (is it only my imagination?), it seems everywhere I go, I see toddlers and littles in elevators, grocery stores, the mall, and cars with devices in their hands and their little eyeballs glued to screens: mom's iPhone or iPad, or the DVD player in the car. 💡 Are we failing to teach our babies and children how to negotiate the "stuff" of everyday life without electronics? I fear we are. Using electronics as perpetual "anytime" pacifiers debilitates them relationally, and reduces their ability to reason and make sound judgements and to communicate effectively. You might think you're getting peace and quiet while you shop. Maybe that's true. But the loss of healthy dialogue and life skills is so steep. Are you prepared for that? Don't disconnect these little years from their future success.

Monitor how much television your kids watch and how much time they spend playing video games; in short, how much time they spend tethered to a screen or other media source. The American Academy of Pediatrics (AAP) has given us some worthy guidelines. According to this organization, children under eighteen months old should have no screen time at all. Furthermore, for eighteen to twenty-four months, they adhere to the old fashioned, but simplicity, of such programs as *Sesame Street.*

For me personally, I say keep your child away from the television and the iPad and all electronics until after two years old.

AAP recommendations for media use by children:[12]

"For children younger than 18 months, avoid use of screen media other than video-chatting. Parents of children 18 to 24 months of age who want to introduce digital media should choose high-quality programming and watch it with their children to help them understand what they're seeing.

- For children ages 2 to 5 years, limit screen use to 1 hour per day of high-quality programs. Parents should co-view media with children to help them understand what they are seeing and apply it to the world around them.
- For children ages 6 and older, place consistent limits on the time spent using media, and the types of media, and make sure media does not take the place of adequate sleep, physical activity and other behaviors essential to health.
- Designate media-free times together, such as dinner or driving, as well as media-free locations at home, such as bedrooms.
- Have ongoing communication about online citizenship and safety, including treating others with respect online and offline."

The AAP also qualifies the viewing time had by young children as "quality entertainment media." (Is there such a thing?) Nevertheless, the lesson here for parents is this: turn off the television and shut down the iPads. Children are able to entertain themselves in the most uncanny of ways.

Families need to be more intentional and proactive about having time around the dinner table. They need to have courage to designate a time—Friday nights, Sunday afternoons, and/or weekdays after 8 p.m.—as a phone- and device-free time.

I struggle to completely separate from my phone, as well. Especially with young adult drivers in our household, and also with just how much of our daily work is contingent upon our abilities to communicate electronically. But there is *possibly always a time and place in our homes worthy of being a phone-free zone!* We need desperately to turn this trend around with our kids. Contemplate this for a minute: we have yet to see the results and outcomes of a generation who has lived their entire life with electronic devices constantly in hand. *What will that study reveal?* If current trends of media use among very young children, and the misuse of cell phones in high school classrooms are predictors, I think there is increasingly a reason for grave concern.

FOR PETE'S SAKE, KEEP TELEVISION OUT OF YOUR KIDS' ROOMS!

Keep television (and computers where possible) out of your kid-do's room at least through the junior high years and possibly in the high school years, depending on your child's own propensity for walling himself off from human contact at home. Yep, that pretty much sums that up. Along with this, don't encourage isolation zones. There's great reason to encourage our kids to have quiet and alone times for either personal reflection or study in their rooms or some other place. But that is wholly different from a pattern of isolation from the family. Bedrooms are wonderful "safe places" of "refuge" for our kids. It is fun for them to make their space their own by picking paint colors, and décor, bedding, and the like. But packing it in with televisions, computers, and other electronic devices changes it from a place of rest and rejuvenation to a place of seclusion from everyone and everything. It turns the bedroom into a place of withdrawal and sequestration, with the potential of disconnecting oneself and facilitating separation from all things family.

I would encourage you, especially when the kids are young, to have "community areas" for their desktops, laptops, and television. Places in the houses that are shared by everyone. Our kids have virtually never had televisions in their bedrooms. And they were sophomores in high school before they had laptops in their bedrooms. On that note, our girls were well into teen years before having cell phones. That seriously decreased the chance of isolating themselves from family in their bedrooms. Shelby was sixteen. Halle and Katie were fourteen and thirteen, respectively, before getting cell phones. I am **not** suggesting that you do the same in waiting until your kids are mid-teens before getting them phones, but I *am* suggesting that you control what is in their bedrooms. I mean imagine ten years of your child's life growing up with televisions, video games, and other electronics in their bedrooms. What family time has been missed in those ten years? What conversations did *not* take place over those ten years? How much time was lost, which can never be recovered? Now imagine fifteen or more years of your son's or daughter's childhood bedroom saturated with electronics. Do the math. What price did you pay, or what did you and your child lose for that seemingly harmless decision?

CHARACTER COUNTS:
TIPS #36–42

When our kids were still young, in their elementary school years, Paul and I decided we needed a family mission statement with three accompanying core family values to help us accomplish our goals as a family. It goes like this:

> "We are a family that nurtures a relationship with God and others and recognizes that relationships are paramount in meeting people's needs though Christ-centered eyes."

> Our core values (not in any particular order), which wholeheartedly support this mission statement, are: 1) pressing beyond the status quo, 2) hospitality, and 3) justice.

Regardless of whether or not you choose to have a family mission statement, know that even if you don't, you *are* leading your family down a path one way or the other. The simple truth about a mission statement is that it acts as a beacon along that path to help you better navigate the road in front of you. It helps you to parent your kids through the filter of what you want to ultimately accomplish as a family. How does that work? Well, when you are making decisions about discipline, or jobs, or where to attend church, or how you're going to spend your money and time, you check it against your mission statement. How does our mission statement inform this decision? Or perhaps when assessing choices already made by either you or your child, how did that decision *reflect* our mission statement?

A company's mission statement will probably include components that relate to that company's bottom line. A mission statement for your business might necessarily include elements that are monetary in nature as well as relational—how you want to treat your employees and coworkers. But typically, family mission statements are character driven. Family mission statements are rarely about how much money you make or where you work, or what material things or professional accomplishments you want to amass before dying. Family mission statements are a tool for teaching character. They teach us character, good character, by giving us a goal to shoot for, a moral compass, a directional sign on the highway of life.

For our family, our accompanying core values are simply character traits that point back to our mission statement. In other words, these character traits are part and parcel of the steps we take, or the way we act and respond, in carrying out our mission statement.

Whether you choose to have a mission statement in writing or not, it doesn't really matter. *It is truly optional.* But teaching our kids character is not! I have shared our mission statement and its core values with you just because for us, that has been a big part of helping us teach our kids that character counts. It's not as if we have read it out loud at the dinner table every night for eighteen years. We reviewed it and reminded our kids of its tenets whenever and wherever we deemed necessary, and we always purposefully incorporated it into our decision making, as much as possible, until it just became second nature.

I think that by definition, a family mission statement is about how our family is going to change the world that we live in. If you know me, you must know my rant: *we are charged with raising world changers.* That has a lot to do with character. If it sounds intimidating, let's break it down. We change the world one casserole, one coffee date, one encouraging word, one volunteer event, one baby hugging minute at a time. When your child smiles and pulls someone in who's left out; when they welcome friends in your home; when they extend grace where they've been wronged; when they take a volunteer shift at their church or in your community; when they hold someone's hand in a difficult time; deliver homemade cookies to neighbors (ok slice and bake are okay if you must); when they bend down in order to see a little one eye to eye to encourage them; that's a world changer. You don't have to fly far from home. You can, and great if you do. But this is not complicated. It's my charge. It's yours. We change the world one person, one heart at a time. And so do our kids. I have already said this once before: This world is ugly parents. Again, let's fight back. How? Let's teach our kids character.

So Tips 36–42 are just that: character traits to teach your children. If you skip all the rest, read this. If you were bored up to this point, please get a cup of coffee and prepare to be engaged. There is an old quote from basketball coach John Wooden (1910–2010), whose success in life on and off the court was phenomenal. He said, "The true test of a man's character is what he does when no one is watching."

Mission statement or not, as positive parents interested in raising positive children, we must agree to be on a mission to teach our kids that character counts. *This is not an all-inclusive list by any measure,* but I feel that the character traits I have chosen to discuss here are ones that in recent years have been *impacted, or in some cases have been redefined,* by our culture. Culture is an important influence on our kids, but your influence as a parent is even more important. Historically, our culture has never been the best teacher of character. It is time as parents, we took back the reins.

Teach Your Kids More about Resilience and Less about Resistance

In our culture today, we sometimes unwittingly (or wittingly) teach our kids to resist not just authority but also how to resist being generous and caring drivers, students, coworkers, and adults. Ironically, simultaneously, these same kids who are hammered with mastering resistance cannot deal with any adversity whatsoever in their lives. Teaching resistance at the total expense of resilience, renders them completely incapable of dealing with any conflict or disappointment that intersects their path.

A school district not far from us, for nearly twenty years, has had a policy in place for selecting the student who is to give the commencement keynote address. The top ten percent of the class academically is invited to submit a speech to a panel consisting of students, administrative staff, and teachers. Whoever among that top ten percent of students chooses to submit a speech must also recite the speech to the panel, or "try out," if you will. Then the objective panel chooses the person who they feel has done the best job in both their speech writing *and* in their delivery of that speech. Therefore, this policy does not conform to the traditional standard among high schools wherein the valedictorian is necessarily, automatically, the keynote speaker. And it was this one particular valedictorian at this particular school who submitted her speech and recited it for the panel, but was not selected. With the blessing of her parents, she went to the local news station and complained on the local news affiliate. She also made a "stink" at school, complaining in both venues that it was a popularity contest only. Yet she did not do this *prior* to delivering her speech. No, indeed, she did not make this complaint *in lieu of* taking part in the established selection process. She only did the complaining and "resisted" the whole process **after** she found out she was not chosen to do the keynote speech at graduation. And I couldn't help but wonder, why in the world did her parents tell her to fight this battle? Would she have resisted this process had she won the speaking spot in the first place? Ostensibly, the answer to that is no. How many of us even remember who our keynotes speakers were? And if we do remember *who* it was, do we remember *what* they said? Not after thirty-five years. I would guess not even after five or ten. Sadly for this student, she will not likely remember much of what was said at commencement, but she will indeed remember her senior year being marred by an incident that could've been avoided altogether if only her parents had been more interested in teaching her just as much about resilience as they did resistance.

The kind of resilience that teaches our kids to bounce back after a loss or a rejection. The kind of resilience that teaches our kids their intrinsic worth so that they don't waste time comparing themselves to others. The kind of resilience that teaches our children how to *not only stand up for others when they are being bullied but also how to withstand bullying.* The kind of resilience that teaches our kids that not everything is about them. The kind of resilience that teaches our kids when to stand and fight and when to walk away. "Choose your battles wisely" (Tip #12) is a timeless piece of advice for parents. It is unequivocally a timeless piece of advice for our kids. But instead, often is the case, we are teaching our kids to resist everything from standardized testing, to teachers, police officers, and other authority figures with whom they have *personality conflicts,* to saying the pledge of allegiance, to not turning off cell phones in public forums (including classrooms and movies). Resilience or resistance. Both are necessary *some* of the time. However, teaching our kids resistance at the total expense of resilience, unwittingly teaches them to be self-entitled, disrespectful, and not diligent in completing work and projects and homework. Resistance is necessary *some* of the time. Resilience is necessary *ALL* of the time.

If you look back over the past 200 years of this country's evolution and study both of these concepts and their place in our history, you will most definitely find a hearty dose of both. But I believe that you will find resilience was indeed in the greatest supply when building up this country into what has made it such a world power. You will see that it was resilience that survived the Great Depression, the Dust Bowls, tornadoes, hurricanes, and many other events that have shaped our history and lives. Resistance was necessary for sure in different stages, in different political seasons, and in wartime. But resilience was present in *all* of these seasons. Resilience is what truly built this country from a vast, unsettled frontier into a thriving, growing democracy. Resilience, not resistance, is what got people back into their homes after the devastating impact of a tornado or hurricane. Resilience is what pulls us through hard times and loss. Not resistance.

Do you want your children to be generous and compassionate adults? I hope the answer to that is yes, but if it's "I don't care about that," then here is another question, "Do you want your children to be successful adults?" That answer is most assuredly, "Yes!" Then stop focusing so relentlessly on resistance and teach them how to be resilient. It will far outlast any other character trait you instill in them, perhaps other than love. *And ironically, do you want your children to be able to resist when resistance is necessary? Well, then teach them resilience.* If they have never been taught how to deal with disappointment, how to choose their battles wisely, how to get up when they have been knocked down—indeed, if they have never been taught resilience, they will surely never know how to "resist" when the time comes for them to do so. In an article entitled "Declining Student Resilience: Serious Problem for Colleges," dated September 22, 2015, Peter Gray, PhD, stated:

"I have done a considerable amount of reading and research in recent months on the topic of resilience in college students. Our students are no different from what is being reported across the country on the state of late adolescence/early adulthood. There has been an increase in diagnosable mental health problems, but there has also been a decrease in the ability of many young people to manage the everyday bumps in the road of life. Whether we want it or not, these students are bringing their struggles to their teachers and others on campus who deal with students on a day-to-day basis. The lack of resilience is interfering with the academic mission of the University and is thwarting the emotional and personal development of students. We have raised a generation of young people who have not been given the opportunity to learn how to solve their own problems. They have not been given the opportunity to get into trouble and find their own way out, to experience failure and realize they can survive it, to be called bad names by others and learn how to respond without adult intervention. So now, here's what we have: Young people, 18 years and older, going to college still unable or unwilling to take responsibility for themselves, still feeling that if a problem arises they need an adult to solve it."[13]

Think about the goals you have set for your children. Or should we say hopes and expectations? Are you teaching them resilience? Because clearly it will be nearly impossible for them to fulfill those expectations or to achieve their own goals if they know nothing about resilience. Clearly once they "leave the nest," and either go to college or to a marriage or a job of any sort, if you have spent all of your parenting opportunities teaching them resistance, but glaringly lacked any lessons in resilience, then they will be part of this statistic referenced here by Dr. Gray. But of more personal interest to us as a parent, our child will not have what he or she individually and personally needs to negotiate the big world that is right outside their front door.

TEACH THEM KINDNESS, NOT TOLERANCE

Teach them to be kind. Is this not one thing we can all agree on? That's the easy part. The hard part is teaching our children to be kind in a world that is drawn to constant comparisons. She has better clothes, cars, houses, parents, spouse, and positions on the sports team. When we fall into the comparison trap as parents, rest assured our kids will do the same thing. If the comparison game is a common practice for you, it will be more and more difficult to teach your children the importance of kindness.

We live in a fast-paced world that lends itself to many people dealing with both hopelessness and helplessness. Pray that your child is kind enough to see that hope and help are within *his* grasp. That can only be accomplished if they are knowledgeable about kindness. And they can only be knowledgeable about kindness if they have been *taught* how to be kind. On the heels of trying to encourage children to be kind, in the last few decades, tolerance has now become a catchword in our country, in our jobs, and our schools. Its original intention, I think, was to express itself as kindness. Why then, I ask, could we not just say, "Be kind"? Kind is not subjective. Kind does not discriminate. Kind is not exclusive. 🗲 The scriptural command to be kind is intended for *all* audiences to be directed toward *all* people. "Be kind and compassionate to one another, forgiving each other, just as in Christ, God forgave you" (Ephesians 4:32, NIV).

Kind is how we treat someone regardless of who they are, what they are, what their religion or political position may be, or whether or not they agree with us. When we are kind, we are not indifferent to the needs and interests of others. Kind does not require us to agree with anyone. It does not require us to pardon a crime. It does not require us to issue kindness at the expense of justice. It simply requires us to be kind to people, whether those people deserve it or not. Kindness. My friend Dan, a pastor, once said, "Tolerance is a cheap and flimsy virtue compared to robust examples of grace, like patience, hospitality, justice, kindness, and love." I couldn't agree more. Tolerance is subjective. In demanding tolerance, are we truly demanding others to be genuinely kind, or is the agenda of tolerance much more cynical than that? I fear it is. I fear that in teaching our children tolerance, we are teaching them kindness with stipulations. For instance, "You can be kind to them only when they agree with your position." Or, "If you do not agree with me, you are intolerant and not deserving of my kindness." Kindness versus tolerance! Kindness is, as my friend eloquently stated, "patient, hospitable, just, and loving."

I don't know about you. But I don't want to be tolerated. I want to be loved. I don't care so much if you agree with me or not, as I do if you care enough about me to listen. And I, in turn, can care enough about you to listen back! Let's ponder for a minute a whole host of ordinary, everyday questions *we all have spoken* in various conversations with friends, family members, or colleagues. "Do you like television?" "Not really. I can tolerate it, but I prefer to read." Or someone has asked me, "Did you have a good day at work?" And I responded halfheartedly, "It was tolerable." Maybe they have asked you, "Do you like your in-laws? Do you like vegetables? Do you like children? Do you like your job? Are you happy in your marriage?" And if you answered, "It's tolerable," or, "I just tolerate them," then I would say that you have a very long way to go before you are eating vegetables with enthusiasm *or* before you are enjoying fulfilling relationships with your job, your family, your spouse, or other people in your life.

No, I don't want to be tolerated. I want to be loved. My preference is to be loved by those close to me and to be treated kindly and with compassion by everyone. I don't want someone to look at me and judge me by my political position, my gender, race, or my socioeconomic status, and then reach the anticlimactic, cynical, and shallow conclusion, "She's tolerable." I want people to look at me, *not through the "tolerance" filter*, but rather through a filter of *kindness and humility.* Teach your children kindness—not the cultural version of that. Teach them kindness, not preferential treatment. Teach your children kindness, not prejudice. Teach them kindness without strings, not kindness with stipulations. Teach them kindness that carries its weight in navigating school, professional settings, church ministry, and personal relationships. Teach them kindness, not tolerance. Kindness will go the distance. It will sustain the beholder through the fast and furious pace of this life journey and render them more success than perhaps any other *relational* trait.

On the other hand, tolerance will assuredly rise up to meet the status quo and keep pace with the absolute minimum effort required in relationships, or in a job, or in framing policy, or in your children fulfilling their dreams. Teach your children kindness over tolerance. One is the real deal. The other is a cheap imitation of how we should truly treat others and how we expect them to treat us.

TEACH THEM FORGIVENESS, NOT BITTERNESS

There are two ways we parent the art of forgiveness over bitterness. The first way is to practice forgiveness ourselves, and the second way is to demand it of our children.

How do we practice the art of forgiveness ourselves? First, we *model* forgiveness for our kids. For instance, we choose not to be bitter about not being selected prom queen when we were in high school. (Don't laugh. Some women still struggle with these issues.) Or we choose to forgive our siblings by allowing ourselves to live a life free of the anger and hurt brought on by the dubious acts of family members. Sadly, family members can be more cruel to one another than complete strangers. We show our children that we are capable of rising above the pettiness and drama that sometimes characterize families or office staff or a church body. We show our kids that choosing forgiveness over bitterness frees us to enjoy our lives, improve ourselves, and even improve our options.

We also model forgiveness by actually saying, "I'm sorry." Do we ever? When I was growing up, no one ever said, "I'm sorry." Not that we didn't have plenty occasion to do so with one another. But no one did. My grandmother who raised me was a powerful, productive, super intelligent

147

woman whom I loved so much, but she was hard emotionally. My grandfather was equally a hard man. I learned so much about life with these two and I miss them even now after all these years. But I had to learn the art of an apology much later in life. And as the saying goes, I learned the hard way. Life has a way of rolling over you like a bulldozer when you are emotionally unequipped to stop it, as I was. I proceeded to fall flat on my face in multiple situations until I learned the importance of being able to say these two simple words: "I'm sorry." Or these four words: "Will you forgive me?" A simple, truthful statement: "I'm sorry for my angry outburst, or for cheating, or for lying, or for not doing the dishes," can move mountains in our life, free up space in our heart to love another person, or help us gain a new perspective on what is important and what's not.

Sometimes verbal forgiveness is unnecessary but should be exuded by our countenance and demeanor. In the large city where I live, a lack of forgiveness is acutely present on the highways and roads. I am pretty sure that my town has the angriest, most unforgiving drivers in the country. Sometimes we need to say, "I'm sorry." And other times we just need to release grudges against complete strangers for driving too slowly or for cutting us off in traffic. Sometimes we have to examine the grudges we hold against people or the world for something that didn't go exactly the way we wanted it to go. Or we have to examine the anger we nurse for something we didn't get—a part in the play, a promotion, a raise. In general, as a parent, if we expect our children to be functional adults, our daily countenance needs to be one that is not a doormat of passivity, but one that is self-confident and forgiving—not holding onto past hurts in a way that prevents us from present success. Had this attitude of forgiveness and apology been more prevalent in my house when I was growing up, I might have made a myriad of different decisions concerning a wide range of personal issues that affected my ability to function in healthy relationships. Neither this book or this particular Tip #38 is about how our childhood ruined us. *No indeed!* It is, and I hope will prove itself to be, a book that allows all of us to perform an honest examination of what values we were raised with and how those values shaped us and our abilities to be joyful and emotionally well adjusted.

The first way we parent the art of forgiveness is to model and practice the art of forgiveness ourselves. The second way we parent the art of forgiveness is to demand it of our children. Our girls attended a wonderful little preschool two days a week when they were young. When one of the preschoolers did something wrong to their fellow classmates, the teacher required the offender to tell the offended, "I'm sorry for _____" and also offer to make amends. In other words, if they pushed Billy onto the ground, they would have to verbally apologize and perhaps offer a cold washcloth for his skinned knee. The wounds, whether verbally or physically inflicted, were not only apologized for, but where appropriate, restitution was made. We adopted similar rules with our girls at home. If one of our girls did something to hurt their sister or their friend, or their cousin, or even an adult, *when we were aware of it*, we required them to say, "I'm sorry for _____. Will you forgive me?" Furthermore, when they were old enough to write simple sentences, we would even have them write, "I will not hit my sister," all the way down the page. Don't get a false picture in your head of our household. It wasn't any different than anyone else's. Our girls were the same as any other toddler, tween, or teen. That's my point exactly. If you have kids, they are going to be hurtful to others at times. It's not only the nature of children to be this way, it's *human* nature. Setting a standard of forgiveness and apology in your family is a key way to produce positive children who are successful and who are able to choose healthy relationships. Not setting a standard of forgiveness will be a contributing factor in their inability to ever find true contentment in their lives.

A word to the wise parents: when we look at either first, ourselves or second, our children through rose-colored glasses, we may never fully embrace the necessity of forgiveness. It's paramount that we understand we are all human and flawed. There is not a single one of us who do not have the inner capacity to either say or do the wrong thing.

Some time in my 30s, long after I had been married and had my children, I had this epiphany. I not only wanted to be remembered by those I love as a tough, persevering, can-do, and intelligent woman but I also wanted to be remembered as forgiving. I had fallen flat on my stubborn face enough times—saw the sadness of my children over my actions—that finally with the help of prayer and the intervention of family members and friends who loved me enough to hold me accountable, I decided I wanted to leave a legacy of forgiveness and grace for my kids to model for others long after I was gone. And with that desire came two simple words in my vocabulary: "I'm sorry."

Forgiveness is a dicey thing. Isn't it? We often like to expound on the impossibility of practicing the art of forgiveness by reciting horrific incidents like the Holocaust or a violent criminal act against someone's child. For many of us, offenses like these are unimaginable. Choosing forgiveness over bitterness is even more so unimaginable in this case. It's hard to wrap our minds around this tall order. I have been floored by stories like Corrie ten Boom's, who after WWII was able to forgive her tormenter from the Nazi concentration camp where she and her sister were imprisoned for hiding Jews in their home. Corrie's sister did not survive that camp. It is equally hard for me to fathom how families forgive their child's killer. But we have all seen or read about these stories of profound forgiveness. In this tip, I am not going to try to convince you that I have all the answers for these devastating and tragic events. Not even! But there is *one* thing I can say with absolute certainty. For those of you who struggle to forgive an estranged parent or a wayward child, or your preacher, or the friend who did not invite you to her party, I would say to you: "In the event of gargantuan cases of betrayal or personal offense, crimes committed against you or humanity, which seem unsurpassable—this *is not the place for you to start* practicing the art of forgiveness." I am afraid you are right. *It will be quite impossible to forgive a ginormous betrayal or hurt inflicted on you by another if you have never practiced forgiveness in the plentiful, lower-level offenses that life offers up every single day.* If we have never forgiven our moms or our dads for not being there for us in the past, if we have not forgiven our best friend for stealing our boyfriend in high school, if we have not forgiven the government for withholding so much money out of our paycheck in taxes, if we can't be graceful to other drivers on the road, *then mammoth personal betrayals, or any higher-level offenses that happen to us or around us will be absolutely insurmountable.* They will almost assuredly break us. They will surely result in acute bitterness and negativity, if indeed we have never practiced the art of forgiveness on any level, *ahead* of such larger tragedies that may beset us.

Personally, I don't think any of us are singularly equipped to forgive a wrong committed to us without the help of a greater power. And that is true whether it is a simple hurt feeling by a friend who failed to include you in a dinner invitation or a grave betrayal in your life that puts you on a downward spiral. For me as a Christian, that greater Power is my Creator. There are so many wonderful scriptures on forgiveness, but one of my favorites is what I have already shared earlier. I quoted this enough for the girls when they were little that it became almost as common a phrase in our house as "What's for dinner?"

> "Be kind and compassionate to one another, forgiving each other, just as in Christ God forgave you"
>
> (EPHESIANS 4:32, NIV)

Unfortunately for us there are no free passes in that verse. It is a simple, easy-to-read, and understandable verse, but not so simple to practice daily. We should view it as a command. A charge for us from God.

And just as parenting is a charge to us, so is practicing forgiveness. We are not always going to do it perfectly, but we should be striving to model it as best we can for our children, and secondly, we should likewise be demanding it of them.

Left to its own devices, the inability to forgive others simmers and then boils over into our lives and everyone around us. This we all know and can agree on. It's never good. You might experience a smug, short-term satisfaction, but your long-term satisfaction is severely hampered. And if you have children, you are modeling for them an attitude that can only end in bitterness. Who wants that for their children? That bitter root can be exhumed and destroyed if only we choose to trade-in the bitterness for forgiveness. When we do that, we really and truly are trading in bitterness for exponential joy and hope. Who wants that for their children? Me! Let's equip our kids to forgive. Let's teach them to choose forgiveness over bitterness.

TEACH THEM HOSPITALITY, NOT EXCLUSION

I have made multiple references in this book to eating dinner around the table as a family. Hospitality raises that bar and asks us to include others in that intimate place. We have had so many people in our house over the years, in all the places that we have lived, that when we move from one place to another, and I walk through the empty kitchen and dining room, I swear I hear the ghosts of guests who sat around our table (with our kids) laughing, sharing their lives and just enjoying each other's company. It truly always brings tears to my eyes. What an incredible lesson this has been for our girls. No doubt as a result of this family core value, they are so accepting and open to having company in their house. As often as possible, they sit and eat at the same table with our friends, with or without other children present. This has helped teach our girls to be engaging and inquisitive. It has taught them how to show interest in others, and inevitably they have discovered how fascinating other people really are.

Here is a tip inside of a tip. If you are single or married, with or without kids, start a guest book. And each time someone or some people come into your home to eat, stay, or visit, or just have coffee at your kitchen counter, have them sign your guest book. My husband Paul mentioned this idea recently, and when he did, I was just sick that we had not done that when we first married twenty-five years ago!

Having guests in our house has always been a joy for both of us. And when we lived in Germany for four years and were not able to be home for either Thanksgiving or Christmas, this presented a golden opportunity to share American Thanksgiving in our German home with our neighbors and friends who typically included German, Dutch, Belgium, Canadians, French, and Americans. We also hosted a Christmas brunch with some of our very best (German) friends. Now every year, our friend Frank sends us this message from across the ocean on Christmas day: "I miss our Christmas brunch."

Along with the dinner table company, it is important to be hospitable to your children's friends. Our house has always been one that welcomes their friends for parties, sleepovers, homework, meals, and perhaps even emotional refuge. I have mentioned that we were an active duty military family. We moved a handful of times. Each time we moved, I felt the pain of not only separating from my own adult friends but also the sweet kids my girls had hung out with for all those years. They had become a part of our extended family, and a part of our home. I made either photo books or home movies and burned them to DVDs, so I could give their friends a permanent memory of that sweet friendship. Having other kids in our house over these years has been wonderfully noisy. Their voices, their drama, their playing, their friendly exchanges, and their conflict resolution has reminded my girls that hospitality helps grow, mature, and cement relationships for the years to come.

I don't know when it began exactly, but at some point our three girls at a very young age started orchestrating "home entertainment shows," particularly at holiday gatherings and birthdays. They were gems. Each year at Christmas they would create a show for us and the visiting parents of their friends, to ~~endure~~, I mean enjoy! Seriously, our friends and I still laugh about this today, and we have video that is precious to remind us of their antics. One year they wrote their own mini version of *High School Musical* and acted out the musical with three of their close friends at that time. Our girls have always been creative and artistic, so they incorporated dancing, singing, poetry, and sometimes utter ridiculousness into their shows. When we had company over for holiday meals, or birthday celebrations, we simply warned them, "Oh, there will be entertainment. And there is no admission cost. It is free. That's the good news." And I have to say, some of those shows were so stinking entertaining and hilarious, gut-busting funny. And the girls absolutely loved performing in their house for family and friends. Being hospitable and making that a core value in our family taught them many lessons. And one of the most important lessons was that they could be included in that hospitality effort. Not just their dad and me. They learned that they had it within their own power to play a vital role in encouraging and interacting with those who crossed the threshold of our front door.

It is not surprising that as my girls grew into teenagers, they started planning their own parties, for instance Friendsgiving (Thanksgiving), Friendmas (Christmas) and Galantine's (Valentine's) parties. They often create menus, decorations, and specials itineraries for their friends to enjoy around our dinner table and in our home. It has always moved me emotionally when I walk through the dining room and see a table full of girls interacting together, laughing and sharing their life dreams and drama, and my daughter right there in the middle of it all, pouring water into their glasses, and love and acceptance into their hearts. As a parent, this has been one of my favorite values to see my girls adopt as their own and execute with passion. It's better than graduating at the top of their class, getting the best job or promotion, or hauling in a bundle of merit scholarships. It is so sweet and rewarding to know that they see their home as not just a place to start and end their busy days, not only as a place to crash and eat but also as a place that has the potential of being a place of refuge, healing, enjoyment, and love for the people who dance in and out of our lives *in all the places of our lives.*

Finally, hospitality is not only something that happens in our homes. When we learn to be hospitable and encouraging at home, then we find it much easier to practice hospitality away from there. Our kids will learn to be hospitable in their school, in their organizational affiliations, and in their college experience *away from home.* It is hospitable when your child is in his classroom at school and allows another person to share their thoughts and ideas. I don't know. Maybe for you, it is a novel idea that listening to other people and letting them share their own thoughts or allowing them to expose themselves emotionally is a part of the definition of hospitality. But it is. My youngest daughter often has other students (friends or peers) confide in her. I think they sense in her a hospitable spirit. One that is willing to listen and not judge, and where possible, provide words of encouragement. What I am describing is a safe place, a *place.* Just like our homes are actual *places* where we practice hospitality, so is the *safe place* that we provide others who just need a listening ear. That is being hospitable. I am not suggesting that your child is always going to be in a situation of listening to or taking on everyone's problems. Certainly not. Mine isn't either. But they will assuredly, unavoidably, be in numerous situations where they are exposed to their peers' problems, their ideas, and their differences. I *am* suggesting that the less hospitable we are in our homes, the more difficult it will be for us to cope with others outside of those walls. When we are hospitable, we are the hosts. Consequently, we learn a lot about others and ourselves because we learn to listen to those we have invited into our spaces.

TEACH THEM TRUE FAITH, NOT RELIGION

Adherence to religion has produced a litany of life casualties; adherence to a set of rules that even the issuers themselves are unable to bear.

> "Now then, why do you try to test God by putting on the necks of Gentiles a yoke that neither we nor our ancestors have been able to bear? No! We believe it is through the grace of our Lord Jesus that we are saved, just as they are"
>
> (ACTS 15:10–11, NIV)

I have often seen religious Pharisees produce casualties. History has surely taught us the same. A spiritual casualty is any person who has been led away from Jesus rather than pointed toward Jesus by a person's behavior who said, "I am a Christian," but acted otherwise. Jesus said, "By this everyone will know that you are my disciples, if you love one another" (John 13:35, NIV).

On the other hand, I've never known a single solitary casualty of faith in Jesus, being acted out in the lives of Jesus' followers seeking truth through grace and humility. Rejection of His teaching? Yes! Unrepented sin? Yes! I have seen the latter two produce casualties. Of course, I have seen religious Pharisees produce casualties. I have seen people who *call* themselves Christians, but don't *act* Christian, produce casualties.

From the Old Testament: "He has shown you, O man, what is good; and what does the Lord require of you but to do justly, and to love mercy, and to walk humbly with your God?" (Micah 6:8, NKJV). Furthermore, "Religion that God our Father accepts as pure and faultless is this: to look after orphans and widows in their distress and to keep oneself from being polluted by the world" (James 1:27, NIV). This scripture in James chapter 1 teaches two ginormous points: One, faith and religion are two completely different things. Religion is born out of our faith, not the other way around. The kind of real, authentic faith we have, or we do not have, determines what kind of religion we espouse. Religion is neither personal salvation nor is it a denomination. It is truly our personal theology. And that brings us to number two. This scripture in James chapter 1 teaches us that the haughty religious leaders of Jesus' days on earth were missing the whole point of salvation, which is this: the heart of an individual must be involved in their decision to be a Jesus follower, not just their head.

Religion is a convenient list of checkmarks. Church✓☐ Tithes and offering✓☐ Sunday school✓☐. (Whatever religion you claim as yours, I am sure you can come up with your own checklist.) None of these things are bad at all. They are indeed all things we can see, feel, touch, and explain with either the naked eye or our own intellect. But we all know as parents, life isn't that certain. It is in fact *uncertain.*

We live and work in both good and unstable economies. We live in peaceful eras and tumultuous eras. We have joy and we have sadness. Sometimes we can explain a situation. Other times we simply cannot. The same is true of nature. Science can go only so far in explaining life on earth. It is a wonderful and incredible tool—science. But when we put all our eggs into one logical basket, we come away disillusioned, and often like the religious leaders of James 1:26 or Hebrews 10:11: haughty, pomp-ous, shortsighted, and self-deceived. We may have all the answers our minds can hold, but a stone-cold empty heart. It's possible therefore that we can be an atheist, not understanding the purity of the commands of Jesus, *or* else we can easily be a religious Pharisee, our heads full of Bible knowledge, but our hearts full of nothing!

If we choose to teach our children first only a legalistic, rule-following religion, or conversely, secondly, if we choose to teach them no faith, no religion at all, then we are *exposing them without restoration.* In other words, we are churning them out in great numbers into a great big world, but we are simultaneously failing to equip them to handle the uncertainty that is sure to envelope them. Exposure without restoration.

The good news is that authentic faith offers us a third alternative. I call it hope.

Most of us have said to our kids or heard it said to them by another adult, "Have faith in me." In other words, "I'm far from a perfect parent—and your future is not etched in stone, or without challenges, but if you trust me, I will help you navigate that journey. Just have faith in me." We are basically asking them to believe in what they cannot currently see. When their life ends, it will be accentuated by a myriad of paths and a myriad of decisions they chose to take and make. As parents, whether we say it out loud or not, we are asking our children to have faith in us to help them go from A to Z. *Yet,* it is such a cataclysmic jump for some of us to instill in them the same kind of faith in our Creator. It's easy enough for us to understand and embrace the truth that we don't know how all of their life is going to play out. It is easy enough for us to expect them to have faith in *us.* So why is it such a huge jump for us to expect they might be more successful, more content, more empowered, more hopeful about their future if we teach them to place their faith in something even greater than us?

So this tip is important for two groups of parents: 1) those who need to teach their children about a personal, individual faith in God versus only a religion that checks off the boxes on major Christian holidays; and 2) those parents who are asking their children to "Have faith in me, your parent, but that is the end of it." Both have their limitations. In the first camp, personal faith demands more. It demands us to be Christlike, which means loving others when they're unlovable. It demands that we exercise humility as our first character trait. Faith demands all of us *not* to "work" for salvation but rather to accept it as the gift that it is, while extending forgiveness and mercy to ourselves and others. Religion falls way short of that.

Likewise, in the second camp, teaching our kids to place all their faith in us, or in human beings, and with the "buck stops here" kind of attitude, actually lowers the bar for them. The bar of success, the bar of contentment. It lowers the bar. Given the frailty of our own humanity, we can only offer our children a limited explanation of why they should do the right thing. Why they should show mercy to others, why they should do the best job at their jobs, why they should not plagiarize or cheat or lie or steal. And when others fail them (and they will), it is way too easy for our own feelings of betrayal, sadness, and anger to usurp the timeless Tip #44, "Do the Next Right Thing." Faith in a God who is all powerful, who is the only One who is the fulfillment of all things to come in our lives, is what will sustain our children through adulthood and to the end of their life—much farther and more efficiently than what will happen if they only place their faith in us.

Even so, our children are indeed going to place their faith in us. It happens the moment they are born, when they are totally dependent on us for food, shelter, and warmth. Whether we demand it or not. Whether we deserve it or not. Whether we know it or not, they are literally wired to believe in us. So give them something to believe in. Model compassion, justice, and maturity for them. And if you will consider it, instill in them a faith in Jesus so that when we fail (and we will), that faith will point them to *someONE* much greater than us who does not fail and is always faithful.

"If we are faithless, he remains faithful—for he cannot deny himself"

(1 TIMOTHY 2:13, ESV)

160

I believe that as parents we have been charged with shaping our kids spiritually, not politically. If you are one who has put all your eggs into the political basket, i.e., if you believe that everything can be legislated, including morality, then you may be tempted to focus your efforts on shaping your child politically versus shaping them spiritually. Are politicians and laws and legislation necessary? Absolutely! But matters of the heart can't be "fixed" with legal proceedings. That is largely the job of parents. In these politically charged times in which we live, we may be guilty of parenting through the lenses of our pervading political views and political agendas, fearful that if we don't, our kids will be brainwashed by the opposition. In reality, if we concern ourselves more with their spiritual growth and development than we do their political formation, it frees us up to parent them more effectively, unentangled by the anxiety that inevitably accompanies politics. Healthy spiritual growth is a much better predictor of their ability to make sound decisions—personal, political or otherwise.

Don't kid yourselves. Your children will put their faith in someone or something—a boyfriend, a girlfriend, job, career, their bank account, hobby, drug addiction, a narcissist person. Human beings are wired to place their faith in whatever they think is going to give them what they need—or perhaps only at best, what they want. As parents we live in a delusional world when we believe that the best course of action with teaching our kids about God is no course of action at all. "Let them choose for themselves," you say. Choose they will. But what will it be? We have a choice as parents. We can offer our children religion. We can offer them "faith in me—the parent." Or we can offer them a third alternative. We can consider a faith in *someONE* greater than themselves. *SomeONE* who offers hope in difficult situations. Mercy when we need to forgive ourselves. Mercy when we need to forgive others. Discernment for all of life's decision. We can offer them faith in God.

THERE IS NEVER AN EXCUSE FOR RUDE

This sure goes hand in hand with Tip #37 "Teach Them Kindness, Not Tolerance," and yet it is different. Rude infiltrates our daily lives and our everyday moments. It typically affects those in our immediate presence. It involves our behavior in the classroom, the restaurant, the driver on the road, and our interaction with family members, friends, and complete strangers we meet in public. Indeed, it *will be* a determining factor in how kind we can be in our life and in our ability to care for others, as opposed to just tolerating them. But it stands alone as necessary character trait for day-to-day living. And given my own strong personality, this has been one of my own biggest struggles in everyday life.

This tip has been "preached" by my husband, the father of my children, since they were able to talk. Never play the personality card as a free pass for fundamental expectations and behaviors. If your child is shy or outgoing, introvert or extrovert, quiet or noisy, they should be expected and required to use manners. They should be capable of looking someone in the eye and have a conversation with them, order their own food, and treat others with respect. When I substitute taught, just the simple task of taking morning role could become a circus. Kids are often not taught simple manners. If someone says your name, a simple "here" or "present" is fine. On the other hand, "Yeah," grunting, or totally ignoring the teacher—none of these are respectful responses. I can't tell you how often I see a small child get a free pass for rude behavior from his parent, who chimes in immediately, "He's shy." I have friends with autistic children who require these basic manners and courtesy from their *mentally challenged* child. Yet, we often struggle to require it from our kids who are not anywhere on the spectrum of diagnosable mental disorders. We live in a world where adults are in such a hurry to get here or there, and are so impatient, that they are often very rude themselves. It's a tall order to expect our kids to use respect and common courtesy in their everyday life when the adults in their lives do not model it.

And while we are on this subject, be wary of the labels you or another person attaches to your kids. ADHD, LD, ODD, the list is endless. Are many of these labels valid? Yes, of course. But the louder we yell this to our kid, *the more they become the label, and the less we expect of them.* The less they expect of themselves. Each child is unique and special—intrinsically and independently of their diagnosis, their labels, their personality quirks. Often, their label becomes their personality. Their label defines them. Sadly, separate from their label, they feel unimportant. Their personality or their label becomes their free pass, their excuse from simple expectations of courtesy and respect. Be on guard, parents.

PARENTING TIP #42:

TEACH THEM JUSTICE

I try to teach my girls that human beings are important—period. In the history of human existence, hundreds of thousands of people have lost their lives due to someone's injustice. In recent years, it was policy put in place by the officials of the City of Flint, Michigan, that failed the citizens of that city. The powers that be insisted the water was okay to drink when actually it was heavily contaminated, and hundreds of people became gravely ill, and some died as a result.[14] Teaching my kids that human beings have intrinsic value is a very opposite message that the culture teaches them. Our culture often teaches our children that one's value is only measured by "What can you do for me? If you can't accommodate my need or if you don't hold a certain lofty position, or if you don't make X amount of money, wear the right clothes, or have the right job, then you have no value." Often policy, personal or public, is a conduit for justice. Therefore, necessary policy should be viewed through the lenses of human life. This kind of policy might have saved lives in Flint.

We have truly always tried to teach our girls to not judge a person's self-worth based on appearances, preconceived notions, or stereotypes. Gather information, I say. Ask your own questions. Get to know the person or the subject matter before opening your mouth. That it is worth something—always. It is the surest way to justice. When our causes

165

become more important than people, then we are likely to jump on any bandwagon that supports our rant, at the total expense of justice. When we do this, we have lost at relationship building. The breakdown of relationships can occur on all levels, personal, professional, and political, when justice is an absent variable in our decision-making process. The ability to show compassion or generosity—two characteristics paramount in personal and work relationships—is greatly hindered. This doesn't mean we teach our kids to be doormats. On the contrary, strong girls equal strong givers. It does mean that when we are considering whether to work late every Friday night, or come home on time and have dinner with our family, maybe we need to consider, in that situation, "policy is hurting my relationship with my kids." This is a dicey subject because it spills over into every area of our lives. There is so much application that can be made in our homes and at our jobs when it comes to the policy versus people discussion and truly examining what is just or unjust in the places we live and work. It is truly about relationships. Policy is absolutely important, everywhere, not the least of which is inside your family home. But for policies to be able to sustain themselves and make positive contributions, they must be encased in strong family or strong personal or professional relationships. Even when policy requires us to hold others accountable, and it does sometimes, we should consider the value of the person whom we are holding accountable, and that should help to inform our decisions and actions, which will inevitably impact them. We should consider justice. This doesn't mean that life is always fair. Heaven knows our kids need to understand that truth and learn resilience. But justice is really in its simplest form, about recognizing a wrong and trying to either right it or prevent it. This is so important in parenting. Moreover, if our children perceive that they are loved unconditionally, then they are more likely to believe that the rules (policies) we hold dear in our household are steeped in justice, that they are there to protect them and to promote their best interests. If we live our lives privately and publicly, both in our speech and action, in such a way that we dole out justice only to a select few, we cannot expect our children to trust the rules we have instituted at home.

Money Talks:
Tip #43

Teach Them about Money

Recent statistics reveal the following facts about debt in American households. As of June 2017, according to the United States Federal Reserve, "America Household Revolving Debt" (i.e., credit card and other revolving debt) is the highest reported amount in history at 1.021 trillion dollars. (Average per household: $15,654.) As of March 2017, "Total Outstanding U.S. Consumer Debt" per household (including housing, auto loans, and student-loan debt) was 12.73 trillion dollars.[15] (Average per household: $131,431.) We know that our country has about 14 trillion in debt, which includes an approximate $666 billion deficit.[16] But what about this latest statistic revealing our personal household debt? How does that figure into our nation's economy? How does it figure into our own ability to secure our future and our children's future so that when we retire we don't have to pick up a job at a fast-food restaurant to make ends meet, or when they graduate from a four-year university, they may do so without debt? Just like with the kindness rule for our littles, if we aren't practicing, then we can't be preaching. As parents we must set the example of paying our bills and living debt free as much as is humanly possible. We cannot perpetually blame our debt problems on the economy or our low salaries or lack of jobs as long as we carry smart phones, pay for cable television, and buy a five-dollar coffee every day. Get on the bandwagon with a monthly budget. It truly makes a huge difference in your personal finances and your future security, regardless of your salary.

It is true that salaries and income among Americans fluctuates more than the weather. My husband and I both grew up fairly poor, by American standards. We did not go hungry by any measure, but pickins' were slim. We did not shop, go to movies, eat out, or have toys. As grown-ups, we make a ton more money than any of our parents or grandparents ever made. We have known plenty and we have known want (not poverty). Because I have lived on dramatically different ends of the income spectrum, I want my kids to understand the value of a dollar and what it means to be a good steward of what you have financially and otherwise. Being good stewards of our income, meager or plentiful, gives us the credibility to expect our college student to actually use a budget software program every month for budgeting *her* meager income. It gives us credibility with our kids when we tell them we are not eating out tonight or we cannot afford to buy *that* dress for homecoming. And it teaches them not only the value of a dollar, but it may well teach them how to put food on their table after you (the parents) are long gone, and they hit hard times in an economy that is sure to fluctuate their entire lives.

And most importantly, unless they are good stewards of their own money, managing it well, and staying out of debt, it is always going to be a struggle for them to give back, to donate, to use the money and resources they have for the good of others who are less fortunate.

I Messed Up:
Tip #44

DO THE NEXT RIGHT THING: IT'S NEVER TOO LATE

M aybe you are reading this book and you are in the latter stages of parenting, or perhaps you have teenagers and you are just reading some of these tips and ideas for the very first time. And perhaps as a result, you are saying, "It's too late for us." It is never too late. The late Stephen Covey authored one of my favorite books, *The 7 Habits of Highly Effective Families*. In that book, he shares a story about a father who wanted to mend his relationship with his daughter, but it seemed no matter what he did, it was not working. Following the logic behind Covey's concept of "building up someone's emotional bank account," the father decided that for thirty days, he would make five daily deposits into his daughter's emotional bank account and, as much as possible, avoid all conflicting language and negative speech with her. For thirty ensuing days he gave his daughter lots of verbal affirmation and also served her with loving actions. His hope was to let go of any negativity that up to this point had characterized their relationship. The response from the daughter was amazing and overwhelmingly positive. She seemed to understand that her dad truly wanted a relationship with her for no other reason other than he actually cared for her. The dad was afraid that he was stepping into this game too late to make a difference in his teenage daughter's life or for them to be close. He couldn't have been more wrong.[17]

None of us get this parenting adventure right all of the time. Not when our kids are infants, toddlers, tweens, or teens, or young adults. We don't get it right all the time, whether we read this book at their birth or wait and read it when they are twenty. But we can always, always *do the next right thing*. My good friend and parenting mentor Carole once told me, "Judy, when you do something wrong, do the next right thing." She was given this advice by her brother years prior to us meeting. She was graceful and encouraging, so much so that she gave me this advice when my girls were very young, and I have never forgotten it. It is applicable in virtually every area of our lives, not the least of which is in parenting. *Just do the next right thing.* Apologize if necessary, or walk out on a temper tantrum, talk it out, be quiet, cancel the plans, remove the obstacle, schedule an outing, stop and take a deep breath, count to ten, arrange to have coffee, invite a discussion. The next right thing is *whatever needs to come next* after either a specific incident (we broke a promise to our ten-year-old about taking him to the county fair) or following a pattern of behavior that has occurred possibly over years (alcohol abuser; years of conflict-resolution avoidance, years of hostility; or estrangement after divorce). Sometimes *the next right thing* action follows something small like losing your temper and yelling at your children at the end of a long day. Sometimes the *next right thing* follows something much larger and more complicated, like disconnecting from your child after a divorce or lying to them about events in your family. In either case, unfortunately, we don't have control over the outcomes or the *results* of the steps we take in doing "the next right thing," but that does not nullify the need for us to do it. If we have any chance at all in rebuilding relationships with our kids, particularly our "big" kids with whom we have become estranged or separated, we have to take the plunge in doing *the next right thing. Doing the next right thing* gives parents a reset button. In a simple situation, it allows us to take inventory of the long, arduous day we have had with our sleepless toddler or our sick ten-year-old, or our ornery teenager, push the pause button and restart our engines. But doing the *next right thing* can also offer a reset button in situations with older children, even our adult children. We cannot erase the past. There is no rewind button. We cannot erase events that have already taken place in our lives and in the lives of our children. But we can make a decision about the future. We can face the facts about the day we have just had at work, or the moment we just had with our child in the car after football practice, *or* we can face the facts of our past, a difficult past that may have left an indelible mark on your relationship with your child. And once those facts are exhumed from the places where we have buried them out of sight (but never out of our minds), exposed for what they are in the light of day, then and only then can we can do whatever is *the next right thing*.

On Being a Family: Tips #45–47

TRAVEL WITH YOUR KIDS

W hy is this a tip? Why is this in this book? I could write pages and pages of why, but there are a few primary reasons why I say "travel with your kids." It is paramount that your children be exposed to a variety of cultures, people, situations, and places. This could mean both fellow Americans as well as people in foreign countries. Remember in grammar school when we learned the definition of a noun? I bet, like me, you can still say it like you did when you were six or seven years old: **people**, **place**, or **thing**. That is exactly why we should travel with our kids. So that we can identify and perhaps understand better people, places, and things. That is to say, people, places, and things that may be a lot like us, and people, places, and things that may be very different from us. Traveling "out of town," maybe just a few towns over from your hometown *or* to Grandma's town, or Auntie's town, or maybe a state over from yours could have a lifelong positive impact on your children. Maybe a different country will be on your itinerary. Each of those geographical locations are going to present golden opportunities for you and your kids to learn from *other* people, places, and things. Twentieth-century American writer Brad Newsham said, "Travel is transformational, the strongest human urge, the thing that keeps us and our world vibrant and alive. It is one's duty to travel, to keep moving, to expose oneself to foreign cultures, foreign landscapes, foreign ideas."

We want our kids to be more accepting of others, to be able to meet people right where they are and start a conversation without undue expectations. We want our kids to be able to gather information on their own and to assess situations *in* their lives for the *rest* of their lives, situations that inevitably involve people, places, and things. The less exposure they have had to people who are different than they are, the more difficult it will be for them to do that.

Another reason why we should travel with our kids is when you get away from your home base, and in a place that doesn't echo all that is familiar to you, as a family, you just naturally bond together. In all of our travel exploits, our family has relied more on one another for comfort, peace, and provision than in any other physical setting. I mean really, when your surroundings are unfamiliar and out of the ordinary, you will cling to the only "ordinary" familiar thing nearest you, your parents and siblings. No boyfriends, girlfriends, best friends, school activities, nothing and no one to get between you and your family members. I know some of you are thinking, *We may be killing each other by the end of the vacation.* Well, part of the vacation fun is enjoying the company of our parents and siblings when everything is going well. But another important element of the family vacation is endeavoring to navigate and reconcile conflict that is certain to arise upon being taken away from your "friend squad" back home and thrown together with just the fam!

Finally, travel teaches us oceans of lessons about foreigners (even those from a different state in the USA), and geographical locations and history. (Yep, **people, places**, and **things**). American writer James A. Michener said this in 1907: "I was once asked if I'd like to meet the president of a certain country. I said, no, but I'd love to meet some sheepherders. The sheepherders, farmers, and the taxi drivers are often the most fascinating people." And another of my very favorite travel quotes from American writer Maya Angelou in 1928: "Perhaps travel cannot prevent bigotry, but by demonstrating that all people cry, laugh, eat, worry, and die, it can introduce the idea that if we all try to understand each other, we may even become friends."

We lived in Germany for four years from 2008–2012, compliments of the United States Air Force. During that time, we vacationed as a family as often as possible. And when my husband was not able to go, that did not stop my girls and me from venturing out on our own. Suffice to say our penchant for travel was exploited all of those four years. It was an incredible privilege to live in a foreign country and therefore have your own home as base of operations for traveling around Europe with relative ease. But it wasn't always easy. One cannot oversimplify the orchestration involved in going from one country to the other on these family trips. There were language obstacles, innumerable etiquette faux pas, and major driving challenges. But that did not stop us from soaking up so much incredible history, culture, food, people, places, and things with gusto. On the contrary, each time we traveled successfully, our travel muscles were buffed up for the next adventure until, finally, we learn to expect adversity in travel rather than fear it. And sure enough, the adversity and obstacles become less and less threatening as our confidence soared more and more. I don't think the obstacles were ever totally eliminated. Some of them maybe. It's just that our excitement, anticipation, and absolute joy outweighed the challenges inherent in traveling, to the point we were more and more able to take the challenges in stride.

I asked my girls for their answer to the question: "Why travel?" Here are their responses. Shelby (twenty-two): "People should travel because it opens your mind through learning more about other people and their culture, which makes you a more appreciative and empathetic human being." Halle (twenty): "My favorite thing about traveling is meeting people." Katie Ann (eighteen): "I love to travel because it's the best way to learn about history and other cultures—it's much different than reading about it in textbooks. It's the textbook in real life."

If you can save daily coffee money for a year, go visit a nearby city for a few days. If you can go without cable television for a year, perhaps a nearby city, *and* a neighboring state could be on your family travel agenda. And if you can go without a car payment for a year, get your passport stamped and visit a foreign country.

Getting out of our geographical comfort zone, together as a family, teaches our children so much about healthy risk taking. Consequently, the impact this can have on their self-confidence, their ability to empathize with others, and their capacity for wisdom is incalculable.

PARENTING TIP #46:
_____

ENCOURAGE SIBLING
RELATIONSHIPS

Cultivate sibling relationships. My parents died quite unexpectedly when I was five years old. Consequently, my sisters and I formed a close bond that contributed to our healing. The past is a good teacher. Paul and I certainly know firsthand the value of our daughters' relationship with each other. Grow your kids together as much as possible when they're young. Think family trips, dinner table conversation, and supporting each other's activities. Our girls have argued over spilled milk often. One constant complaint for a long time used to be Halle borrowing her sister's clothes and never asking. Or Katie complaining about doing the dishes one too many times. Or Shelby demanding that everyone be ready to go out the door to school the minute _she_ appears, even though _she_ literally had only been up for ten minutes at the time of her demand, while everyone else had been up for an hour or more. We would often say Shelby, our oldest, was "large and in charge," at least in her thinking. This served to irritate her sisters repeatedly. Nevertheless, they are fiercely protective of one another. When one of them did not make a tryout or audition, the other two were ready to confront whoever they believed to be responsible. Usually, the most upset among them were the two _not_ involved in the tryout or audition. They know more about each other than their closest friends. They are ready at a moment's notice to supply emotional support on demand.

One morning while alone in a quiet house, I had a chance to examine Halle's and Katie's homemade gift for Shelby who was slated to leave the house that weekend for college. I sat on the floor in my upstairs hallway staring at this homemade gift, crying like a baby and wondering when in the world did these three human beings grow so close *and* grow up at the same time? My thoughts turned to dinner table, family vacations, dance recitals, theatre shows, sports, church, volunteering, and traveling. We had been doing all of these things with the girls, together in tow *for so long, that right under our noses, unwittingly,* they became who they are now: close, tight, forever bound together with a deep-seated love for each other and a profound respect for one another's dreams, hopes, and aspirations.

DO EAT DINNER AROUND
THE TABLE

S hoot, for *AT LEAST* three times a week. Sure, it's hard. "We've got this, and they've got that." Well, I have a Crock-Pot, a (make ahead) casserole recipe, and a calendar. And *now*, there's this contraption called an "Instapot"! You can and should make this work. Statistically, eating dinner around the table together is one of the best parenting tools ever! No, not kidding! Columbia University conducted a survey regarding this rather mundane family activity and its monumental impact on a child's decisions.[18] In a statement accompanying the survey, Joseph A. Califano, Jr., founder and chairman emeritus, said this:

"Over the past 18 years, The National Center on Addiction and Substance Abuse at Columbia University (CASAColumbiaTM) has surveyed thousands of American teens and their parents to identify situations and circumstances that influence the risk of teen substance abuse. Why? Because a child who gets through age 21 without using illegal drugs, abusing alcohol or smoking is virtually certain never to do so. What we've learned is that parents have the greatest influence on whether their teens will choose not to use. Our past surveys have consistently found a relationship between children having frequent dinners with their parents and a decreased risk of their using drugs, drinking or smoking, and that parental engagement fostered around the dinner table is one of the most potent tools to help parents raise healthy, drug-free children. Simply put: frequent family dinners make a big difference."

Eating meals around our table has always been one of our favorite times to talk together (often everyone at the same time), laugh, share, eat, discuss, create, pray, and spend precious time getting to know each other. My youngest daughter's favorite dinner table activity is to go around the table and share something we appreciate about the person sitting next to us or to go around the table and share a way each of us showed gratitude or was helpful to someone today. Katie Ann gave this game a very simple name. She will often ask, "Can we play *Go Around the Table*?"

Dinner do nots: Don't eat in front of the television. Research shows not only is this unhealthy, increasing your chances of stroke and heart attack, but it also discourages conversations with your children.[19] Don't let the kids isolate themselves in their bedrooms during dinner. Make this an opportunity for family engagement. Since my girls have left for college, I am glad that this was a family value we cherished and maintained all these years. And likewise have a family night. Maybe you can play board games or watch a movie together, but put away electronic devices for a couple of hours one night a week and just spend quality time together.

We had two of our nieces spend a large portion of several of their teenage summers with us when our three girls were still very little. When these girls were with us, we incorporated them into family night on Friday nights, including Friday night family dinner. I had totally forgotten about this, until one day at a family Thanksgiving celebration, my grown niece Anita said, "Remember Friday nights were always family nights. We went out to dinner and Amy and I got to take turns picking the restaurant or the meal." Both of those nieces are grown women now, and our daughters are young women themselves, and what do they remember the most?

Not what presents we bought them for every birthday party or Christmas morning (although there are some stand-out gifts among those), but rather they remember those Friday night dinners, riding down the road together, with the noise level in the car off the chart (two teenagers and three little girls), laughing and sometimes arguing our way all the way to dinner and back home!

Our daughters remember the routine of eating virtually hundreds of meals together around the table in our dining room. But I just want to drive home this crucial piece of advice: eat dinner around the table at home as much as possible. Believe the masses of experts, and nonexperts like me, who tell you that the benefits from this ONE simple activity alone can make your family life outlandishly joyful. Apparently, it also impacts high school graduation rates, kids saying no to drugs and addiction, and youngsters' ability to stay out of trouble with teachers and other authority figures. Eat. Dinner. With. Your. Children. Find a way to make this work. It is a proven tactic for success in bringing your kids closer to you emotionally as well as grooming them for success in life.

I Promise, They Aren't Going to Break: Tip #48

Quit Treating Your Children Like Porcelain Dolls

Your kids are more resilient physically and emotionally than we give them credit. Don't exacerbate the situation. You know the one. They come home crying on your shoulder about the teacher or the other student or the bus driver who made them feel bad. Or someone made fun of the way they spit when they talk or how they roll their tongue. You have a choice in that moment to commiserate with them or tell them they can just ignore it. You could say this teacher won't be the only teacher or boss or coworker who hurts your feelings. This peer won't be the only one who makes fun of the way you roll your tongue when your talk or the way you run. And who cares? If we teach our kids that their worth is not contingent upon what others think about them, *only then can we expect them to have the ability to take the words and actions of others in stride.* If we tell our girls to persevere through a tough class with a tough teacher, we might say stuff like: "Do your work regardless. Push through it regardless. Ask questions regardless of whether or not this teacher gives you a warm fuzzy." In this way, they learn to deal with adversity at a time in their life when the stakes are low. If we tell our kids to not take it personal when one of their friends jokes around with them about how red in the face they get when it is hot outside, then we send our kid the message: "Really, this does not matter. What *does* matter?" And hopefully, that rhetorical question will reset their focus.

The thing about porcelain dolls is that they break easily. We want our kids to have a soft side, but we want that soft side to be for others, not so much for themselves. What do I mean by that? If they are always a victim, then they cannot clearly see the position or plight of another person. The other person's position and plight will always be over shadowed by your own child's sense of helplessness. Don't raise helpless kids. Make them strong. When you do, they will be not only safer and more secure in their own skin, but they will have the ability to empathize with others and be compassionate in a way that is life changing to themselves and to others. I know this tip is suspiciously close to Tip #36, which reminds us to teach them resilience over resistance. And to that end, you may be accusing me of literary redundancy. (Is that a thing?) But alas, that just goes to show you how serious I am about raising strong children, who are able to fend off the monsters of criticism, self-doubt, and fear, all of which render decision-making paralysis. On the contrary, kids who have been raised with a healthy practical dose of "can do" *along with* love and acceptance, minus the coddling, are more apt to make positive decisions.

Don't Drop the Parenting Ball: Tip #49

PARENTING TIP #49:

JUST PARENT YOUR CHILD

I would submit that *the problem isn't as much poor parenting, as it is un-parenting!* This is not a popular topic. However, in many cases, there are classrooms full of students who are un-parented. There are sports teams and dance rosters full of un-parented children. And often, these sports teams, as well as school principals' offices, are inundated with the ranting and verbal, if not physical, attacks of unscrupulous parents. I call these kids simply *un-parented kids* who themselves apparently have *un-parented parents*. For purposes of this lesson, *un-parented* is defined not by orphan status or by the absence of parents in the home, but *rather*, un-parented is defined here as a *pattern of behavior* displayed by an individual who utilizes no filter with his actions or words along with maintaining a pervasive attitude of disrespect for others and an intense focus on only one's self and one's own immediate interests. When I was a "dance mom," back in the day, our team of moms would have made for a very boring reality TV show. We all got along well and truly liked each other. Our daughters were spot on the same way. They were, not because they were perfect little angels, but rather because it is what their moms demanded of them. On the other hand, I knew of one "dance mom" connected to a different dance studio (yes, indeed a grown woman) who would send out bitter and callous text messages to her fellow moms in the group that were rude, insulting, and unbelievably childish. Lo and behold, guess who else did the same thing with her fellow dancers on the team? Her daughter. What a shame. A grown woman, a mother, a wife, educated and living in an upper-class neighborhood (lest you think that this sort of thing discriminates among income demographics), ♀ who apparently was never taught as a child how to respect herself or others. And she is passing on that legacy to her daughter. Why? Because she can. We all know stories like this. But when are we going to stop and do a self-examination and ask ourselves the hard questions? What areas of my life and attitude need improvement? What are my triggers? What pushes my "rude button"? How is this counterproductive to getting what *I* want, as well as meeting the needs of others in my family and in my relationships?

Recently, a message thread went on for days on our local neighborhood website community page. There had been an incident at the local high school that got a few parents of students talking about how it was handled by staff. They took to social media, specifically our neighborhood's community site, to let others know how they felt about the situation. *Whatever value the original thread may have had at the beginning of the conversation was totally obliterated and obscured by about the fiftieth comment.* At this point, the parents (yes, adults) were shouting names (albeit electronically) at each other, launching verbal missiles at their supposed foes with words like "pathetic" and "brainless." They were full up verbally attacking whoever on the thread opposed their view. The irony of the whole thing was that the original concern involved a student at the school who apparently had anger issues. This student had made a threat and ostensibly posed a security issue for students and staff. The parents, on this point, wanted the school to expel him, but also lamented over a perceived lack of communication from either the district or the school about the student in question. But these **same** parents who were so concerned about this boy's anger issues—*clearly these parents themselves had pretty serious anger issues.* Like I said, it wasn't so much rather they were wrong or right. At this point they were so rude, slanderous, and unprofessional that wrong or right was downright fuzzy. What they were modeling for their own kids was how *NOT to resolve conflict.* They chose instead to model methods for destroying another person's self-esteem, self-confidence, and self-worth. This they were doing quite well. I call this *UN-parenting.* I can only imagine the impact this kind of behavior, displayed by grown men and women, can have on the behavior of their own children.

Parent your child. Be present in their lives. *Be with them, not just around them.* Spend quantity time with them that is enriched with quality. The old saying "quality over quantity" is totally lost on a child who has an absent father or an absent mother—for *whatever* reason.

Have meaningful conversations with them. In those conversations, outline your expectations: 1) be respectful of those who are in authority over you; 2) be respectful of yourself, and others; 3) be on time; and 4) do you work at school; and at your job.

Now let's break all that down a little bit more.

Authority has become a "dirty word" in our American culture. Authority. All my life I have had people in authority over me. Bosses, parents, grandparents, teachers, security guards, customer service agents. Yes, there are and will *always* be people in authority over us. It is foundational—brick and mortar—in a free society, a defining trait that actually sets us apart as a civil society and distinguishes between the two: an uncivil and barbaric society versus a civil and peaceful one. No doubt about it, in our American and world history, authority has been abused. We often lament over a news story of a teacher in a school who took advantage of a child, or the history of the plight of African Americans who were abused by those in places of authority both in the church and in our society. But alas, to say, "Because there are people who have abused their authority and exploited others, we should *never* respect authority," is a dangerous precedent to set with our children. Especially if your child is surrounded and engulfed by plentiful amounts of every material item known to man. If I used the example of what happened to African Americans in America or Jews in Nazi Germany as an excuse for *my* children to buck all authority, that would be pretty offensive to African Americans and

Jews. To categorize *my* privileged kids in the same boat with the former is preposterous. Really? Our kids *should be taught to recognize the difference* between proper authority and abusive authority, not throw them all in the same pool together.

Your child may find themselves in a place of authority in the future. What then? Wholehearted disregard for authority figures based on the actions of the perverse is certainly unfair to a teacher who is full of integrity or an honest law enforcement officer whose sole interest is in keeping peace and protecting your family. People generally agree that they want to live in a civil and peaceful society, but there are widespread differences in opinion of how that civility is achieved—particularly as it relates to the need for respecting those in authority. That is manifested in how we parent our own children when it comes to this same issue. We need to teach them that respect is both a noun and a verb.

Slandering those in places of authority does nothing to bring about real change. Opposing them with civil and professional protest, expressing your opinions, either through action or the written word, pragmatically and emotionally with passion that goes to the heart of the matter, is wholly separate from ranting, complaining, lashing out, rioting, being violent, hurting others, not showing up for your duties, not carrying out your responsibilities, or acting illegally. It's paramount as parents that—if we expect and hope that our children can enjoy relative peace and safety in their future and in their homes—we teach them this very important distinction. Teach your child the importance of respecting sound authority. Just parent your child.

Parent your child to be respectful of themselves, and don't tolerate helplessness. Teach your child: "be your own best friend." Not in a narcissistic way. That is the opposite of what I am saying. *IN fact*, people who are *not* respectful of themselves, who constantly seek the approval of others, who compare themselves to everyone, those individuals tend to be very narcissistic. I mean how can you be anything but narcissistic when your concern is wholly centered on yourself and what others think about you? Teach them to be confident in themselves and to take self-initiative. That's what I mean by "teach them to be their own best friend."

You do this by encouraging their imaginations early on in life, reading lots of books that offer different points of views and perspectives, while exposing them to potential growth and success opportunities. We do this also by being present in our child's life and giving them appropriate touch and appropriate affirmation along with accountability and responsibilities. We do this by not taking all the shame and guilt from our own life experiences and laying it on the backs of our children. We do this by modeling self-respect for them. I have seen so many young girls in schools, in churches, and in friend circles whose helplessness and neediness far outweighs their ability to discern between the respectful and disrespectful intentions of the opposite (or same) sex. As a result, they allow themselves at a very young age to be labeled, touched inappropriately or bullied or mishandled, emotionally or physically, by boys or girls alike. They don't respect their body and often make poor decisions about their bodies, all because they struggle with self-respect.

Teach your child to respect others, but to also respect themselves. Model self-confidence and a "can do" spirit for your child. Make this a way of life for both of you. We are our own best advocates. Not a coach, or a teacher, or a lawyer, or a minister, and ultimately not our parents. And if you are a Christian, we know this: "But the Advocate, the Holy Spirit, whom the Father will send in my name, will teach you all things and will remind you of everything I have said to you" (John 14:26, NIV). We also have the encouragement of Hebrews 7:25: "Therefore he is able to save completely those who come to God through him, because he always lives to intercede for them" (Hebrews 7:25, NIV). Even more so, this scriptural truth should inspire us as Christians to stand up for ourselves and ask the appropriate questions of others that concern our bodies, and our jobs, our relationships. Teach your children to respect themselves. Just parent your child.

In our American culture, we often send the damaging message that self-respect and self-confidence can simply not coexist with respecting others. That self-confidence cannot coexist with courtesy and even generosity. This is hogwash. And it is a lie. I think it is true that the line between being respectful of others while advocating a just cause for ourselves or others can sometimes be blurry. For instance, when a car mechanic lies to me about some repair that needs to happen with my car, is it for me to respect him while at the same time explaining my position? Yes, it is. In fact, I can best hope that he will think twice about lying to another woman about an unnecessary and expensive car repair when ONE woman takes the time to professionally and respectfully rebuff him and his deceitful claims with appropriate and necessary inquiries. On the other hand, given his already shady and immoral character, evidenced by the fact that he willingly lied to me about an unneeded repair, if I blow up at him and treat him rudely and with the exact same disrespect he afforded me, I can assure you with a ninety-nine percent certainty that my response will, in his immoral and shallow mind, all but justify his original deceitful and lying behavior. He will most likely add to that some further speculation about the female gender and their inability to control their emotions, that indeed he was right all along about women. I don't need to fuel the unrighteous emotions and cantankerous position of such an individual by acting like a raging maniac. I need to be different. We need to teach our children this is indeed what separates us from the uncivil. This is indeed what separates the reasonable from the unreasonable person—our abilities to stand up for ourselves and others with dignity, sound words and judgement, and deliberate, rational action. Teach your children to respect others. Just parent your child.

Be on time. Ironically or not so ironically, most of the children I have known who are never on time are daughters and sons of parents who are never on time. Being consistently late to everything sends a negative message about your abilities and your personal or professional interests. It is also rude and shows a marked lack of respect for the event organizers, your school administrative staff, your boss, or your children. *Whatever* you are late for. We all run late occasionally. There is plenty out there to drive a wedge between us and our destination. I live in the fourth-largest city in the country, so traffic comes immediately to my mind. But when we are consistently, perpetually late, it tells others, "I don't care enough about you or this activity to give it my best," which includes being on time. Being on time is an impressive attribute in a world that has adopted more and more of a lackadaisical attitude toward others and their needs and desires, whether that is a loved one, our boss, our church, our school, or our work. You may ask, "Judy, who cares if I'm late as long as I show up and perform my duties accordingly once I am there?" The answer is this: "There is a person or persons who care that you are late. They are your teachers, your pastor, your boss, your mom, dad, child, or spouse. They are your loved one, your significant other, your neighbor, your peer, your project manager, your student. They are likely one of those people. *They* care that you are on time." Teach your child to be on time. Just parent your child.

Do your work. Whether your child is a full-time employee or a full-time student, we need to teach them that their best is always demanded. Not perfection, not a total lack of errors, but their absolute best. Too many students see school as a perfunctory task that is painstakingly necessary on the path to liberty and freedom. They don't often understand that education is itself a portal to liberty and freedom. And doing our job well in school can maximize their chances at good-paying jobs and solid futures. Fail at this, and the road ahead of them is even harder, the chances of their success even slimmer. Parents, truly the stakes are low when they are at home with us and in school. Typically, they are responsible only for themselves—not a spouse, a child, or a set of coworkers. The stakes are low now! Ostensibly, everything is at their disposal: an education, parents who feed and clothe them, and hopefully the resources to succeed in school. Once they graduate, the stakes are much higher. And once they get involved in long-term relationships or have children, the stakes get higher and higher. Stay in school. Get them help if they need it. Utilize your counselors, principals, and peer groups all to your child's advantage. This. Is. The. Easiest. Season. Of. Their. Life. We all know it gets harder and more challenging, professionally and emotionally, as they age. Teach them to stay in school and teach them to do their very best while there. Just parent your child.

There is no such thing as a "good kid" or a "bad kid." These are both derogatory terms. Let me explain. I think it is as misleading and confusing for us to say to a child "you were good today," as it is to make the negative statement to them "you were bad today." Both are nonspecific in nature. *IN* fact, if you tell a child he is "good", it just follows that the opposite of that is "bad." Their resulting emotion is just as confusing as the original statement. Why? Because there is an assumption: "Apparently, when I am *not good*, I am just plain bad." Just as we need to be specific in our praises or our accolades: "I really appreciate how you did the dishes without being told tonight," or, "You did a great job turning in all of your homework this week," we also need to be specific in our criticisms. It's a waste of time and counterproductive to say, "You were bad today." Tell them where or how they performed below expectations. Both are necessary in order to parent effectively.

It's important to note that this section isn't about labeling kids "good or bad." Kids are dealing with enough labels as it is. Children are not a project or a sports team or an organization. They are individuals with beating hearts and blood coursing through their veins. This section is about recognizing that when we choose *not* to parent our child, in other words, when we choose only to be a peripheral presence in their life, scooting in and out of their world only as time or desire allows, never having life-giving conversations with them about real-life issues, never teaching them any conflict-resolution skills, always looking for the fastest and shortest way to the finish line, **then** we run a high risk of sending un-parented children out of our homes. Out to where? To school, to sports teams, to jobs, to marriages, to the voting booths, and out on their own, totally unprepared to be a part of the progress around them and unable to recognize what it takes to succeed individually or in a group.

While I believe there is no "good or bad kid," I do believe there is such a thing as an *un*-parented kid. What parent ever holds their newborn baby in their arms and says, "I hope you are always late, hate school, irresponsible, and disrespectful to everyone trying to help you or keep you safe"? Said no parent ever! Yet, we sometimes struggle to prioritize these very important tenets in the success equation for our children. Teach your child to respect authority, to respect themselves, to respect others, to be on time, and to do their job well. Just parent your child.

CALLING ALL PARENTS: TIP #50

PARENTING TIP #50:

None of Us Gets a Free Pass

What? None of us gets a free pass? What in the world?

How do you stop a fast-moving train? This is hard. How can one possibly tell a mom (for instance) who was abused as a child, or neglected, or a child of an alcoholic, "When it comes to parenting your child, you don't get a free pass"? Just because you endured all of this hardship, unfortunate as it is—as difficult a childhood as you might have endured—you still have to parent your children effectively. Sorry, no one gets a free pass. That's a hard thing for us to grasp. It is hard to say it out loud and even harder to resign ourselves to it as a basic virtue of mothering and fathering. Parenting is just stinking hard in any and all circumstances. But how much harder for someone who grew up with the worst of circumstances, or with the craziest parents who ever lived, or who endured a bad marriage, for them to be told, "You don't get a free pass, either"?

We have an inherent responsibility, a moral charge to raise positive and emotionally functional children to the very best of our abilities. We can't throw them to the wolves. Even if, as children, we were thrown to the wolves by those charged with nurturing *us*.

We also cannot accept the "luck of the draw" attitude for our children.

"Sorry, you got me as a parent. Therefore, you get what I got. No encouragement. No firm foundation. No unconditional love. I didn't get it, either."

We cannot adopt the attitude of despair and then use that as an excuse for not raising children with purpose. Addictions, deaths, betrayals, divorces be damned. We will not assign a life of nothingness to our children simply based on the events of our past. When we have a child, we have a chore—a charge. We can choose adoption, which is a wonderful opportunity for someone else to parent, or else, we can keep them as our own and surround ourselves with a village of people, hopefully another parent, and pour into them love and hope and lessons. So that they in turn can pour into others, maybe children of their own, love and hope and lessons—maybe. And just maybe in so doing, we can stop that seemingly endless cycle of abuse or mistrust or anger that has defined our own past. No one gets a free pass.

My friend Mindi* was abused by her husband for years in the *shadow of their church steeple* where they attended faithfully week after week. He served as a ministerial volunteer there, and on the outside everything seemed okay. Together they had four children. Mindi was lost and alone as many of us have found ourselves at one time or another in that pit of despair and abandonment. She became addicted to hard drugs, and at some point she sunk to perhaps the lowest point in her life. With the help of a friend and no doubt the *grace God in her life* (my emphasis), she made her way past addiction, and amazingly all the while restored and maintained a close relationship with her children. But what really amazes me about Mindi's story is she never makes excuses for her own choices throughout that season of her life. She acknowledges fully the toll that addiction to drugs took on her life. Even though, ostensibly, she was driven to that point of despair by another person. Even though she was betrayed not only by that same person whose vow was said out loud years prior, in the presence of witnesses, to love and care for her, but

---

* Mindi is not her real name.

moreover, the betrayal she felt by her religion and perhaps her own personal faith—still yet, in her healing process, she knew that her personal restoration involved restoring her relationships with her children. One part of this was apparently apologizing to them and not making excuses for her own culpability. She candidly told me how she stood in front of them on one specific occasion when they threw the proverbial stones at her, and she was frank and honest with them about her shortcomings, while at the same time not relinquishing her authority and influence in their life in that moment. Wow! I think it would be so easy in our humanity to bow out of their lives. And when they say, "Well, Mom, you did this and that wrong," it would be so normal to disengage and to abdicate your parenting influence to chance. The guilt and shame of our past can be overwhelming to the point of debilitating us totally as parents.

My friend Mindi is one of the brightest, most successful mothers I have ever met, and one of the reasons that this is clearly true, is the fact that in spite of circumstances beyond her control, and in spite of the hurt afflicted by her ex-husband, she never gave herself a parenting pass. If anyone could, she could have. Her kids have asked her the hard questions, and she has answered them with brutal honesty about her mistakes, and all the time without verbally blasting her ex-husband.

When I look at Mindi, I see a rock of perseverance. She is someone who says with humility, "I made mistakes, big ones; I've also been forgiven. I was given a clean slate. I loved my kids through the nightmares of my life and because of that, in spite of my mistakes, I still had and have expectations for them. I still hold them accountable for their own actions." She never ever once adopted the attitude of 1) "Because of what I did," or 2) "Because of what someone did to me, I can't raise my kids to be different, and I can't be expected to know what's the *next right thing*" (Tip #44). She used the common sense with which God endowed her, and she surrounded herself with a few capable, loving, and supportive people. She applied her intellect and old-fashioned tenacity to her situation, and she made it. Because of that truth she embodied—"parenting is not all lost just because I had a bad hand dealt to me"—she has a loving, respectful relationship with her children, one that I greatly admire and respect. Who wouldn't? And she has found joy in her second marriage to a man who treats her exactly as she should be—with devoted love and respect.

In the case of my friend Mindi, her first marriage did not survive and she was divorced. You may choose to stay in a difficult marriage as you continue to parent. I'm not here to counsel you one way or the other with regard to the question before you (perhaps): "Should I stay, or should I go?" (Unless you are being physically or sexually abused, then you should go and take your children with you. Seek immediate help and shelter from your abuser!)

Each woman's circumstances and the position taken by their spouse contribute to that outcome. It is easy for us to be judgmental about another person's decision to stay or to not stay in a difficult marriage situation. Whatever we decide is the best for us and our children, it is absolutely paramount that no matter what, we choose to thrive as a parent. We must not fall victim to the attitude that "because of my difficult marriage situation, I can only parent one way—the wrong way." Nope! We have to decide that we will continue to love our children enough to not shrink back, but still maintain expectations for them. In Mindi's mind, she had been given a parenting charge the moment those children became hers, and therefore the bar was raised far above her trials and hardships and bad choices, far above the abuse of her marriage. Whatever you decide to do in your marriage, stay or go, you must always choose to parent effectively, and as much as possible without laying upon the backs of your children the drama and hardship that has unfortunately been yours to experience. If there is any hope, whatsoever, of stopping this junk from moving into the next generation, if there is any hope of shaping a different experience for our children, then we have to decide that we must and can rise above those unpleasant and sometimes horrible circumstances, out of the darkness that plagues us, into the light of believing that we truly can parent with a positive, effective, purposeful plan in spite of it all. I have only to consider my friend Mindi to know this can be done.

My sister Cindy was separated from our other sister and me when

I was about ten years old. Our parents died in a fishing accident when I was five, and my sisters, six and nine. We moved in with our maternal grandparents. Life was hard for them, and it was even harder raising a teenage orphan who had lost her way the day our parents lost their lives. So fast-forward four years from the deaths of our parents, my oldest sister now thirteen, and off to a teen boarding home (not school) she went. I'll skip a lot of the sad details of her time there. Suffice to say, she witnessed a lot of suffering and sadness in her new home. And life without her back home was emptier. We grew up with hardworking, God-sent grandparents. But nurturing wasn't really a part of the equation. Perhaps Cindy, in her "home away from home," had even less. I can never be sure of that one way or another. And certainly, no one has their suffering tally sheet out. That only hurts the bearer of the tally sheet. Keeping score of our hurts doesn't do anything to move us forward. That being said, Cindy has never been one to compare her less than amiable circumstances to mine or anyone else's in an effort to "one up" her suffering. Her journey from being orphaned at nine to her marriage and having children and becoming an empty nester, and then a grandparent has been fraught with both hardship and hope. It has been a path filled with grief, grace, forgiveness, anger, confusion, reconciliation, and ultimately light. I know it wasn't always easy. I know because she has been candid in sharing with me the lows and the highs, the mistakes and the corrections, the failures and the success of both marriage and parenting. No one is perfect. We are only perfected by the truth of our circumstances. And then only as much as we are able to acknowledge, adopt, and apply those truths in our life to our current situations. The ability to do this in her adult years has carried her to a place of redemption and joy that really can't be explained fully without truly acknowledging the impact of people who have surrounded her, affirmed her, and accepted her along the way (Tip #1), 🐦 who themselves (wittingly or unwittingly) have been mere extensions of the faithfulness of God.

The thing is, either of these two women could have chosen negative parenting, no parenting (Tip #49), or just apathetic parenting over positive parenting. And indeed, these women might tell you they did exactly that, at some point in their journey. But given their personal circumstances of a lack of role modeling, a plethora of emotional setbacks, and many moments of poor and misguided judgments made against them, it would be not surprising to any of us if they *never* steered themselves onto a path of positive parenting. But nevertheless, their emotional setbacks, their moments of bad judgement, their bad choices (even those resulting from the bad choices of others), they owned the consequences of *all of these.* Where necessary they sought forgiveness and reconciliation. Where necessary, they sought counseling, friendship, and support. Where necessary, they got on their knees and prayed that God would stand in the gap for them, that He would indeed overcome their past, and make His presence known in *their* presence. And by doing these things, and by slapping their name on their past and owning all of the "crap" that spewed itself relentlessly into their future, they were able to *not* lay it all onto the backs of their children. And if momentarily they did do this, they recognized their actions in doing so and sought a different alternative. Ultimately, they took strides in their life and in their parenting that moved them and their children from darkness to light, and from despair to hope.

At some point in their journey, at some point in their healing, they chose to parent with intention, with dedication to positive principles, and most importantly they chose to parent with the belief that they were *worthy* to parent their child with purpose, that they were *worthy* to love their child and to be loved by that child.

It is a broad spectrum of parents present in this world. And with that cast of characters comes a broad spectrum of circumstances, backgrounds, and income variables—the marginalized and the privileged. But I can only stand by my tip that *no one gets a free pass.* It must be the lens through which we parent. If it is not, then the results will be exactly as you might expect. A repeat of all that was lacking in our lives, a repeat of all that we suffered ourselves. Believe that you can parent with purpose and positivity and with hope in spite of whatever may have tragically befallen you as a child or adult. Therein lies hope and healing for all of us.

It's a Learning Curve:
Tip #51

FORMAL EXPERTISE NOT REQUIRED; GUMPTION AND GRIT ARE A MUST

When we have children, there is no textbook really, no exact blueprint for constructing positive children. There is no educational degree required, no bachelor of science, no master's, nothing. There are no prerequisites for becoming a parent. It does not matter our education level, family money, political affiliations, or lack thereof with regard to any of these things. Parenting is the one place, perhaps the only place, where we all begin on an even plane. The playing field is absolutely level when it comes to becoming a *new* parent. That should put us *ALL* at ease. This is important to understand and grasp for a couple of reasons. First, we should all understand that becoming a parent is new to all of us the first time around. All the college degrees in the world, and all the money, high-paying or low-paying jobs, will never fully prepare you for this journey. There isn't a seminar or a birth class that can fully describe what it is like to become a new mommy or a new daddy. Not one.

So never feel left out or alone in that way. Never feel like you have been given less than what is required for rearing children. Although we know that our pasts contribute to our feelings of worthiness and ability, and yes, our knowledge base contributes to success, still we start parenting in the same place as everyone else. With a brand-new baby! <u>We all get the same incredible chance to do something different than anything that we have ever done before.</u> We should definitely understand and embrace the idea that learning and acquiring more information on parenting is very important, but we should likewise understand and embrace the idea that "I am capable and up to this task." Just because you have no formal training in parenting doesn't mean you can't. That is the springboard for undertaking this new adventure and for embracing any tip you find in this book. I. Am. Capable.

In a similar way, I undertook this project. While it is true I have a college degree, I am neither a child psychologist nor a certified family counselor. I **can't** write a book on parenting with the subtitle: "Based on my twenty-two years of professional counseling with teenagers and their families…" But it doesn't mean I can't undertake this project. We have personal experiences that bring us to places of understanding and insight. In terms of education, there is also "the school of hard knocks," "the school of trial and error," and "the school of learning from our experiences." And for many of us there is our journey of faith. All of these latter events and circumstances will meet you at the starting line as you set out on this uncertain path of parenting. And it was largely those life experiences and my own personal parenting experiences that began me on this book project. My formal education was not a hard and fast contributor at all.

For sure I have some citations and references in this book. I hope they are relevant and helpful. I did my best to reference articles and statistics I felt had integrity and that cause us to think progressively. But there are very few. Not only am I not a psychologist or counselor, but I am neither a statistician nor scientist. There's a lot of fabulous literature out there on the brains of children and how they work. Boys and girls. I have several in my personal library that I have enjoyed reading and studying. But in the end, the tips you read in this book have been born out of twenty-two years of personal heartache, sacrifice, joy, and love raising my own girls alongside my husband and parenting partner, Paul.

These tips are born out of literally thousands of conversations with my own children *and their friends*—at the kitchen table or in the car or at an event or activity—with regard to every possible subject under the sun concerning the current issues of children and teens. Our own kids are a plethora of research data. In the course of writing this book, my daughter shared with me a story of one of her peers at her high school. This seventeen-year-old girl, along with another female student the same age, travel to *out-of-town cities* partying with their mothers at local bars, drinking shots of liquor. This is their chosen mother/teen daughter activity, which they enjoy most. Another close friend of my daughter's, a seventeen-year-old girl, was involved in a sexual relationship with a guy who was very verbally abusive. Suffice to say he was not good to my daughter's friend, but she felt like she had to sleep with him in order to keep him on her good side. And if you think this is an isolated situation, think again. I have known countless girls who felt like having sex with their boyfriend was a condition for sustaining the relationship. And the stories go on and on. Students and teens, who are struggling with pornography or drugs (including marijuana) or boyfriend/girlfriend drama on levels that in the least-case scenario serve as serious distraction from their current main "job," to attend school successfully, but in the worst-case scenario leave them disillusioned, maybe pregnant, or betrayed, lost and no solid direction in their life. Yes, that's *my own* research. And there is no formal, bibliographic citation for that. *But I certainly have not been able to discredit any of this informal data collection as I continue to check it against more formidable sources.*

It's simply a result of being invested in the lives of my teenagers and their friends that has rendered a wealth of insight *into the lives* of my teenagers and their friends. Along with that, I have been involved in volunteering in children's and youth groups for years, and I have volunteered or substitute taught in junior high and high school for the past decade. And we all have access to this "research." This doesn't require a top-secret security clearance badge. It is right at your fingertips—a ton of data on current issues impacting our kids in their culture, their schools, their churches, and in their communities. And if **they** constitute a sample group, then this data has much to contribute. Formulate your own sample group. Start talking to your own small children, and definitely talk to your big kids, high school and college. Start talking to your parent friends and to their kids. Start talking to teachers, other educators, and ask your pediatrician questions. Talk to youth pastors and program leaders and coaches. Start comparing notes. You will be like me, inundated with data and research. Does it make me or you an expert on parenting? No, I seriously doubt that. But it certainly makes us more informed. And it is truthful data, no second guessing the source or its veracity. It can inform us as parents and mentors of a child as to how heavily they are influenced by today's fast-paced, busy, social-networking-addicted, sexually charged culture wherein they live and function.

Most of us will never, as long as we live, forget that moment our first child was born and laid across our chests, in our arms. If you were like me, you were overwhelmed with a sense of wonder. How in the world? And you were also at some point overwhelmed with the question: "What now?" Yes, indeed, what now? As I said before, there was neither a college degree nor a great parenting book that brought us to that point of becoming a new parent. It was just old-fashioned physical intimacy. Life is not always a level playing field for everyone. We know that is true. But being a new parent is pretty darn close. Don't spend too much time laboring over your lack of book knowledge. You can and should utilize great books and studies to add to your knowledge base. You can and should have a wonderful pediatrician in your corner. But being a parent or a child mentor, more than anything, requires a whole lot of heart knowledge. It requires a whole lot of *gumption and grit*. It is not for the faint of the heart. Where is your heart when it comes to parenting? Is it aligned with what is best for the child you love and cherish more than all the books and training and college degrees the world has to offer? If your answer is yes to that question, then I think you've got *the gumption and the grit* for undertaking this *wild and crazy but exciting* parenting journey. `

Loosen Up, People: Tip #52

CLOSING THOUGHT:
HAVE FUN WITH YOUR KIDS

When I was child, my favorite pastime with my sister Lori was play-ing either "house" or "school." And that is exactly what we called it. "Hey," we would ask each other as soon as we arrived home from *real* school, "do you want to play house or school?" We were usually play-ing the role of mom, each of us with one child—this represented by our respective dolls given to us by a sympathetic and merciful aunt. Frankly, we were raised by very hardworking grandparents on a fixed income, so toys were a precious commodity. I say these dolls were merciful gifts because one doll was missing a leg, and the other had a pockmark in its face and I'm pretty sure was missing toes or an arm. Yeah, nowadays all of us donate lots of "old" toys. You know the term "gently used"? That is the worthy standard for donating from our households, right? Well, I think it's safe to say that Lori's dolls and mine didn't fall into *that* category prior to their being donated to us. We did not care. At any rate, we were more than happy to parent these less than perfect dolls and overcome and adapt to their shortcomings. We simply pretended we had disabled children. Imaginations like that served us well in the years to come.

But…back to playing house. We would insist, in our grown-up voices, that our husbands could be so self-serving. We would pretend to be very worldly and know everything there was to know about rearing our child and being married and running a household. And the "husbands" (we never had anyone actually "play" this part) were always in absentia. (Sort of like the character in a drama series who is talked about a lot but never seen.) The upside to that angle is we could talk about the husband as much as we wanted, and of course in our minds we were always right and they were always wrong. We would get on our ~~bicycles~~, I mean, in our compact cars, smoking our candy cigarettes (remember those?), drive to the ~~barn~~, I mean, the grocery story, then come back and put our babies down for naps. And when one of the armless (or legless, I don't remember which) babies would wake up from their naps, then I would go to my own ~~bedroom~~, I mean, my own house, to go about my own household business before aforementioned imaginary husband was due back home.

Now I am pretty sure that all of you feminists out there are shuddering as you read about this seemingly patriarchal world of housekeeping that my sister and I so easily conjured up in our minds. But remember, we lived with our grandparents. Our playtime—our imaginary world— reflected the real world in which *we* lived. Suffice to say, I grew up and became a federal law enforcement officer and kicked my fair share of bottoms, so you can breathe a sigh of relief.

But the point I want to make is that some of you are still playing "house." You are all grown up now, at least in a chronological sense. You perhaps have married (or not), and finally, you've had children of your own. But you're *still* just playing house. You haven't truly stepped into your role as a mother or a father. You are too busy at work (or at play), or far too busy with your life away from your children (work, ministry, hobbies) to truly parent that child. On the contrary, you have relegated that responsibility to one or more entities other than yourself: day care center, Xbox, grandparents, iPad, the other parent, the youth pastor, the school— you get the idea. Getting married and having children is not in the same life success category as buying a new car, landing your dream job, buying your dream house in the suburbs, or being famously successful at your work. All of these latter endeavors are just a grown-up way that we play house. None of them are necessarily wrong, by any means. But if they usurp your role as a parent, then you're no different than that little nine-year-old girl riding her bike to the ~~barn~~, I mean, the grocery store, while ~~smoking~~, I mean, eating a candy cigarette. Being a parent is much more formidable than all of these other "things" we do.

Mothering and fathering is much more intimate a gig than any show in which you have ever been the star. We should approach parenting this latter way, in the *here and now*—ostensibly without the façade of our jobs, our house, our "stuff," our portfolios, and without the façade of our personal successes or failures, and even without our own sordid past hanging over our heads. *These are all filters through which we parent—sometimes unwittingly.* They offer input undoubtedly in more ways than one. But *if* all of that were stripped away from us, *and we had only our children*, how would we teach them what is important in their lives and how would we show them unconditional love along the way? In order to march out of the family home with confidence and capability when the time becomes necessary, kids need to realize that they are not the center of the universe, but that nevertheless, they are indeed a priority in your life.

So here is my last parenting tip in this book, and it's an important one. I know that with parenting there comes a lot of high expectations for us and it can be stressful and challenging. I did not give any parent a free pass (Tip #50) for that in this book. So this last parenting tip behooves all of us to see and maintain perspective. Remember this:

Tip #52: Have Fun with Your Kids

Establish family traditions. Go to the state fair together; have family dinners around the table. Read books at bedtime. Sing songs in the car. Remember Tip #31 and be playful wherever you can. Take time for family vacations, special holiday traditions, board games, bikes, walks, and cuddles on the couch. Let them pile up in your bed for a few minutes at bedtime to talk about everything under the sun. (Our big girls *still* do this.) Or pile up in their bed. Laugh out loud together. Share inside jokes, family text threads, music, books, friends, and family. Share your heart. Let them in your world and thank God when they let you in theirs. 🔔 Look straight into their eyes and remind yourself that they are a gift from God that you have been given for only a short amount of time. Like a vapor, this time comes, and it goes so quickly. Love them deeply. Treasure them always.

ENDNOTES

1   Covey, Stephen R. *The 7 Habits of Highly Effective People: Powerful Lessons in Personal Change.* New York: Simon & Schuster, 2013.

2   Woodham, Chai. "Why Kids Are Hitting Puberty Earlier Than Ever." *US News and World Report,* April 17, 2015.

3   Coulson, Justin. "The Problem with Exposing Kids to Sexual and Violent Content," Institute for Family Studies, January 24, 2015, ifstudies.org/blog/the-problem-with-exposing-kids-to-sexual-and-violent-content.

4   Krebs, Christopher P., PhD, Christine H. Lindquist, PhD, Tara D. Warner, MA, Bonnie S. Fisher, PhD, and Sandra L. Martin, PhD. "The Campus Sexual Assault (CSA) Study," NCJRS. December 2007.

5   Wong, Alia. "Why the Prevalence of Campus Sexual Assault Is So Hard to Quantify." *The Atlantic.* January 26, 2016. https://www.theatlantic.com/.

6   USA DOJ Office of Justice Programs, Bureau of Justice Statistics. By Sofi Sinozich, BJS Intern and Lynn Langton, PhD BJS Statistician. Washington, D.C.: Bureau of Justice Statistics, 2014. "Rape and Sexual Assault Victimization Among College-Age Females," 1995–2013.

7   Covey, Stephen R. *The 7 Habits of Highly Effective Families: Building a Beautiful Family Culture in a Turbulent World.* New York: St. Martin's Press, 2010. Pages 201–243.

8   "The common-sense census: Plugged-in parents of tweens and teens." Northwestern University. Center on Media and Human Development. December 2016. https:/www.commonsensemedia.org/ sites/default/files/uploads/research/common-sense-parent-census_ executivesummary_for-web.pdf.

9   "New ASHA Survey of U.S. Parents: Significant Percentages Report That Very Young Children Are Using Technology." *ASHA.org.* May 8, 2015. Accessed January 19, 2018. http://www.asha.org/.

10   Rainey, Dennis, and Barbara Rainey. "Passport2Purity Project." Accessed January 20, 2018 https://www.bing.com/c?IG=581162BE 10994477BB81A81360C49941&CID=230F41DD922B6BB410624 AA093846AB1&rd=1&h=JCJjKrNOdXPH9u3NhwZgagIeYyFmR Fxa8FLOw6TdCkc&v=1&r=https%3a%2f%2fwww.christianbook. com%2fpassport2purity-project-kit-dennis-rainey%2f9781602006874% 2fpd%2f127171&p=DevEx,5506.1.

11   Gardiner, Stephen. "The Student Cellphone Addiction Is No Joke." *Education Week.* April 26, 2016. Accessed January 22, 2018. https:// www.edweek.org/ew/index.html.

12   "American Academy of Pediatrics Announces New Recommendations for Children's Media Use." *AAP.org.* October 21, 2016. Accessed January 22, 2018. https://www.aap.org/.

13   Gray, P. "Declining Student Resilience: A Serious Problem for Colleges." *Psychology Today*, September 22, 2015.

14   Dingle, Adrian. "The Flint Water Crisis: What's Really Going On?" *American Chemical Society*, ACS Chemistry for Life, December 2016, www.acs.org/content/acs/en.html.

15   LaMagna, Maria. "Americans now have the highest credit-card debt in U.S. history." *Marketwatch.com*, August 8, 2017.

16   "Budget Outcomes for FY 2017." Https://www.cbo.gov/topics/budget Accessed February 5, 2018.

17   Covey, Stephen R. *The 7 Habits of Highly Effective Families: Building a Beautiful Family Culture in a Turbulent World*. New York: St. Martin's Press, 2010. Pages 47–49.

18   "The Importance of Family Dinners," VIII. A CASAColumbiaTM White Paper, and QEV Analytics, comps. Columbia University, A CASAColumbiaTM White Paper. The National Center on Addiction and Substance Abuse. September 2012.

19   DELISTRATY, Cody C. "The Importance of Eating Together." *The Atlantic*. July 18, 2014. https://www.theatlantic.com/.

BIOGRAPHY

J udy McCarver has been married to Paul for 25 years. Together they have parented three lovely and capable daughters. Judy has a Bachelor of Science in Criminal Justice and a Master of Public Administration degree. Her professional career has included being a Special Agent with the Drug Enforcement Administration (DEA); a Social Worker in Children's Protective Services; and serving in the military. As a volunteer in ministry for over 25 years, her leaderships roles have included teaching the bible, key note speaking at women's retreats, acting as interim director of a children's ministry, and co-leading in youth ministry. She was also instrumental in helping to reorganize the small groups data base at a large church with multiple campuses. She has trained and coached small group leaders as well. Most importantly, she has a passion for equipping parents with the tools necessary for raising world changers. Her favorite hobbies are traveling, reading, writing, and helping all people, regardless of their personal faith experience, to better understand timeless scriptural truths along with the practical application it holds for their lives. You can follow her at judymccarver.com